THE APPRENTICE WHO STUTTERED

THE APPRENTICE WHO STUTTERED

John Newbury

To Jene
from
J. F. Newbury

14-3-2011

HALLMARK PRESS

Published by Hallmark Press International Ltd
34 Lambton Court,
Peterlee,
County Durham
SR8 1NG

Typeset by TW Typesetting, Plymouth, Devon

Printed by CPI Antony Rowe, Eastbourne

I dedicate this book to my son Aaron
whose enthusiasm encouraged me to write it.
I hope that in years to come it may inspire him
to discover the pleasures of travel that have been such
an integral part of my life.

CONTENTS

LIST OF ILLUSTRATIONS

Foreword

Peter Mole, Nautical Director of the Port of London Authority

When spending time with John Newbury, whether as a shipmate, sitting in his garden, or through these pages, one thing is certain. You are unlikely to become bored.

In a collection of personal reminiscences spanning over 50 years the reader can be carried back to a way of life that is now in many ways long gone, while also being reminded of the constants of our existence.

The steam trains dramatically pulling into Bournemouth Station have been replaced by clinical electrics devoid of character. The bustle of the London Docks with feverish cranes endlessly carrying all kinds of cargo between ship, dockside or lighter with stevedores labouring through the smoky mist has been replaced by the orderly presence of Canary Wharf and the Docklands Airport. The five-hatch cargo ship with heavy lift derrick, a maze of wires and winches and distinctive company funnel gives way to vast container ships passing their boxes in anonymous estuary terminals. The mildly genteel dinner as immaculately uniformed officers enjoy steward service and starched white table linen gives way to self-service snatched in a duty mess without the time to shed working gear or enjoy a leisurely chat.

Fortunately not everything changes. The challenge for a young person aspiring to overcome whatever difficulties to attain command of their own ship remains. The allure and romance of foreign travel is still there. The comradeship of living and working closely with others continues to attract. Great satisfaction can be felt from effectively coping with the demands of seamanship and throughout it all the ferocity of the elements are a frequent reminder of the place of humility in our lives.

When on board with John Newbury the impact of his enthusiasm for life was ever present. It might be in his sheer delight when his favourite sausages were on the breakfast menu or in the early hours of the morning when cold and wet in the bow of a cableship struggling with wind, tide and tiredness to persuade a recalcitrant submarine cable to behave. As a natural ship's master and consummate seaman I remember sharing the great sense of satisfaction when completing a long and complicated operation in the extreme heat of the Arabian Gulf, while his vital role displaying the highest standards of leadership during the Falklands conflict is much admired by those who know the details. Whenever we shared hair-raising moments and there was a need for clear control the stutter disappeared!

While driving his staff to high levels of performance he was always concerned for the welfare of the individual, and no one did more to train and develop his ship's company. Our last professional meeting when he returned from a stint on a venerable ship based in Panama was one when I expected to hear about the problems of keeping the ship seaworthy. Most of the time was spent as he described the fundraising his team had been doing in supporting a local orphanage!

Turning the pages of heritage and snippets of a rich personal story will doubtless give pleasure to all who chose to do so, on a global journey from a busy Hampshire railway platform to a peaceful bucolic Dorset garden.

1

EARLY DAYS

As the train pulled into Bournemouth Central Station there was the usual cloud of steam emitting from all around the engine, which I remember was a Merchant Navy class locomotive; appropriate I thought for this the first leg of my chosen career. The air was heavy with the smell of steam and oil and people bustled here and there. Father had helped me secure the services of a porter to put my heavy bags in the luggage van, for which we gave him a shilling. I kissed my mother and two sisters and shook hands with my father before boarding the train. Picking my seat by the window I put my folded copy of the *Telegraph* on it to reserve my place. With great commotion the train started to move out. Mother and the girls were crying and Father was waving his trilby as I leaned out of the window waving my cap, part of my smart new uniform with flashes on the lapels to indicate my rank as an Apprentice Deck Officer.

I can remember that scene as if it were yesterday. Times and customs have changed a lot since then. Steam has given way to electricity and I doubt if you could find a porter let alone a luggage van. If there was one I would be loath to trust my bags there today. It was 1959 and I was a seventeen-year-old youth embarking on a monumental journey by myself. I had signed indentures with Ellerman and Papayanni Lines of Liverpool for a four-year apprenticeship. The previous week mother had taken me to Southampton to buy my kit, which to my astonishment had cost my parents over one hundred pounds, a princely sum in those days. The Company had sent us a list, which was so comprehensive it even listed the number of handkerchiefs, socks, underwear, hairbrush and a housewife, which contained sewing and darning kits. This of course was in addition to both blue serge and white tropical uniforms and my uniform cap with detachable white covers. There were white tunic shirts with detachable collars and fold-over cuffs and two pairs of black uniform shoes with shoe cleaning accessories.

Only a few months before I had been a carefree student in sixth form, happily drifting through the education system, when I attended a careers exhibition that rekindled my thoughts of travelling to far off places and all the romance that a life at sea conjured up for a spotty faced teenager.

I had for as far back as I could remember wanted to have a career at sea. At sixteen I had applied to join the Royal Navy but failed the medical because I stammered. I had been plagued with my stammer since the age of eight.

My parents were at a loss to explain how suddenly I had difficulty in forming certain words. It wasn't until I was in my forties that I realised the cause of my stammer was from seeing my Grandmother having an epileptic fit. I had come in from school full of youthful bounce and energy only to discover Nana, as we called her, lying fitting on the floor. I had always been very close to my Nana and seeing her lying there like that came as a terrible shock to a young boy of eight. I remember running from the house, desperate to find my mother. I wondered around the streets for what seemed eternity before Mum found me. I never told her what I had seen but just shut it from my thoughts, locked in my subconscious mind.

Suddenly at school I started having difficulties. My teacher was less than supportive and I recall the painful humiliation of being made to stand up and read in front of the class. My tongue had suddenly a huge knot in it and I just couldn't get the words out. When I tried to explain I was told that I didn't know the word and was made to stand in the corner for lying. Fortunately I was fairly popular at school and to the other kids my stutter wasn't such a problem. This passive bullying did more to discredit the teacher than me.

Schooldays became painful until my parents took me away and put me in a private school. They must have found it difficult and I will always be grateful to them for making the sacrifices to find the fees. It took many years for me to conquer my affliction but I was determined to do so.

I can still remember that Navy Doctor telling me that with my stutter there was no place for me in the Navy, and that I was wasting everybody's time. With his words ringing in my ears I went home determined to prove him wrong. If the Royal Navy wouldn't have me then I would try the Merchant Navy. After all, hadn't Sir Francis Drake, Raleigh and Frobisher all been merchant seamen?

My main hobby for years had been sailing and I had for several years been a member of the Christchurch Sailing Club. I hurried home that day from that careers exhibition full of thoughts and aspirations of a life in the Merchant Navy. My parents had always been very supportive to us kids and Dad helped me write letters to a number of shipping companies. Some old friends who haled originally from Liverpool had recommended Ellerman & Papayanni Lines, and I was ecstatic when I received a letter inviting me for interview.

That journey to attend the interview seemed interminable for a seventeen-year-old youth travelling by myself, as it took at least eight hours each way, travelling by train, via London, but it was worth every painful minute, when a few days later the acceptance letter dropped through the letter box. I was to be a midshipman in the British Merchant Navy on a starting salary of ten pounds per month, which was equivalent to the cost of a return journey by train from my home to Liverpool. I was lucky, in those postwar days, that the Merchant Navy was treated as one of the armed forces by British Rail who offered a considerable reduction to our fares.

I had started my journey from Bournemouth rather than Christchurch as this was the fast train to Waterloo where I would travel across London by taxi to catch the sleeper from Euston to Liverpool. Dad had given me the money for a meal on the train and I felt very grown up walking into the dining car, resplendent in my new uniform, and being shown a seat. Catering on British Rail in those days was very good although as I was soon to discover very expensive for a midshipman on £10 a month.

I must say that eating soup out of a bowl on a jolting train was never easy. I was very impressed with the silver service and was amazed at the way the waiter was able to balance against the movement of the train whilst using both hands to serve the food. I can remember having roast pork with all the trimmings, including crackling and apple sauce. I managed to get to London where another porter helped me secure a taxi and loaded my bags whilst offering an outstretched hand for his tip. It was obvious that London charges were different to suburbia, and as he looked disdainfully at my offered shilling I was intimidated into doubling his tip. 'Bloody thieving rogues them porters,' said the taxi driver, although he wasn't averse to accepting *his* tip when we arrived at Euston.

Having been shown my sleeping compartment I was surprised to find that there were two bunks and that my travelling companion was already bedded down for the night. 'I hope you don't snore lad!' was his only greeting before emitting sounds that would have been more at home in a piggery. I was so filled with excitement and some trepidation of what lay ahead of me that I doubt if I would have slept much anyway without the farmyard noises from the other bunk. As we pulled into Lime Street Station I was already up and dressed even though I had at least a couple of hours before my appointment at head office. Having spent yet another two shillings on porterage I found a café where I tucked into a magnificent breakfast. At seventeen food was very much a driving force in my life and as Mother said I could eat like a horse.

Having presented myself at the Superintendent's office I was instructed to take a taxi (under the guidance of the hall porter who this time didn't expect a tip) to Toxteth Dock where my ship the SS *Maltasian* was loading timber. I was lucky that the Bosun was strolling along the deck and spotted me standing forlornly on the quayside surrounded by my bags. He dispatched a seaman to assist me and show me to my cabin with instructions to report to the Chief Officer straight away.

I had a quick look around the cabin, which was to be my home for the next few months. There were two bunks a chair and a small settee against the wall, which I was later to discover was called a day bed, and those walls were to become bulkheads, the ceiling a deckhead and the floor the deck. Looking at the two bunks I wondered if I was to share the cabin with another midshipman. Well that would mean company, I guess.

The Chief Officer Mr Pedley welcomed me onboard and told me that another apprentice would be joining later. I was to get changed into my working gear and report back to the Bosun. Dressed in a new spotless white boiler suit I ventured out on deck. With a laugh in his voice the Bosun sent me under the guidance of the young seaman who had helped me earlier, down a hatch into one of the holds where dockers were loading timber. My appearance caused great amusement amongst the dockers who called out 'Blimy it's the White Tide man!' and 'Omo washes not only clean but bright, Omo adds bright, bright, brightness'. This was my first taste of Scouse humour.

The timber, beautiful beech wood from Greece, that was being loaded had been brought in on our ship from the Mediterranean and discharged onto the quay only to be reloaded for onward transit to our next destination, Glasgow. Each parcel or assignment of timber had to be marked with water-based paint to ensure that the consignments were kept apart. There were buckets of paint of every colour and with huge paintbrushes we made lines across the stow of planks before the next parcel was stowed on top. It wasn't long before my lovely white boiler suit was every colour of the rainbow. We hadn't been at it long before my mentor said 'come on, it's smoko time,' and led me out of the hatch to the crew's mess where I was offered a mug of steaming tea that was as black as treacle. It tasted like treacle too as it was laced with a large spoonful of condensed milk. Good manners made me drink it but I vowed not to accept another cup of mess room tea. We returned to the timber marking until lunchtime when I was told by the Third Mate to go and shower and get changed for lunch. This involved putting on my full blue uniform with studded collar and cufflinks.

After lunch it was back down the hold with more separation lines to be painted. We had to work quickly as the dockers were on piecework and wouldn't hang around. I made some excuse to return to my cabin at smoko time, as I couldn't face another mug of mess tea. As I entered the cabin there was another lad there. We instantly connected and were to become good friends. Although this was his first ship Clive had been to pre-sea school and his Dad was a captain in the company which meant that he was a lot more knowledgeable about ships and the sea than me. This was to save me falling into many of the pits that new apprentices fall into. I however had to get back to my paint pots and we didn't meet up again until five o'clock when the dockers finished.

That evening after a sort of high tea, because dinner wasn't served in the homeport as many of the officers went home, Clive and I started getting to know each other. That was until the Third Mate came in and told us that the Officers still onboard wanted fish and chips and it was our duty to get them. It was dark as Clive and I ventured ashore (not in uniform I must add) and went in search of a fish and chip shop. Toxteth was a pretty rough area in those days and a few years later was to feature in some pretty fierce fighting between the police and locals, which became known as the Toxteth Riots. I was very glad to have Clive as company. I guess that I had lived a fairly sheltered life until then and was very glad to get back to the safety of our ship.

I was born and raised in Christchurch, a small town with historic links going way back to the days of the Vikings. Christchurch harbour is one of the prettiest little harbours on the South Coast and had been my playground as I grew up. It is sheltered from the South and West by Hengistbury Head, and a sandy spit encloses the harbour from the Southeast. Because of its location near to the Isle of Wight it is blessed with four tides a day and a maximum rise and fall of only four feet. The harbour is edged with reed beds and marshy inlets and is shallow and ideal for boating. Today there may be several thousand boats in the harbour but in those early post-war days there were but a few.

My parents owned a beach hut on the sand spit that Dad had built and we spent most summer weekends and holidays there. When I was about eleven Dad bought me a boat, well it was really for the family but the girls weren't very interested and I guess I monopolised it. It was a fourteen-foot salmon punt with a flat bottom that made it virtually uncapsizeable. Of course it was heavy and never intended to be fast, but it was safe and gave me thousands of hours of fun. Each autumn Dad and I would row it up the harbour to a slipway just down the road from our house and it would be kept in our back garden. I would rub it down and give it a new coat of paint, and one year, under Dad's guidance, I built on a little foredeck and a locker in the stern. Dad showed me how to calk the seams and then we coated the bottom with pitch. That boat taught me a lot about boat craft. One day Dad took me to one of the local boatyards where he purchased a new piece of rope for a painter. The owner of the yard spliced an eye in the rope for us. When we got home I unpicked the splice to see how it had been done. When he saw the splice in pieces Dad was rather displeased but after I had reassured him and had remade the splice he bought me a book on knots and splices that I still use today.

That boat was everything to me, from pirate ship to the Golden Hind sailing around the world. The harbour had magically named places like Clay Pool and Steep Banks, Lime Kiln Creak and Blackberry Island. Mother Seller's Channel had acquired its name from a famous landlady of one of the harbour side pubs who was renowned as a smuggler. The reed bed hid many channels where a smuggling boat could hide from the Revenue Officers, and I knew them all. I rigged a mast and put leeboards on the punt, although it was not built for sailing, but she would run nicely before the wind. I would watch the boats from the Christchurch Sailing Club as they raced up and down the harbour and imagined that I was one of them. My favourite boat was a beautiful gaff rigged jack yard topsail sloop of twenty-six feet long, called *Ianthe*. She was the Commodore's boat and had been in Christchurch since before the turn of the century (19th that is). She looked just like a miniature Victorian yacht, in fact that is exactly what she was. Never in my wildest dreams would I believe that one day I would own that handsome vessel.

We sailed from Liverpool about four days after I had joined bound for the Clyde and Glasgow, my first foreign port! As we sailed up the Clyde we were called to harbour stations ready for berthing. Clive went forward with the Mate whilst I went aft to assist the Second Mate. We didn't have hand-held radios nor telephones in those days, just the tannoy system for relaying orders from the bridge. The Second Mate sent me to the bridge for berthing instructions. Because of my stutter, when I got stuck on a certain word like *to* (silly that such a small word could cause me such grief) I would substitute a similar word, but with nautical jargon this could get me into real trouble.

As a youth I once went into a tobacconist's shop with friends to buy some cigarettes. There was a cheap brand called Will's Wiffs which suited our pockets and I stood in front of the assistant asking 'Please can I have ten W . . . Ten W . . . Ten W . . .' The word just would not come out. 'Oh damn it! give me ten Players please.'

I arrived on the bridge and approaching the Captain blurted out 'Second Mate's compliments sir but is it starboard side as well.' 'What the hell are you gibbering about lad?' came the retort. I just wanted the deck to open up for me. Fortunately the Third Mate came to my rescue with 'I think he means, is it Starboard side to, sir.' (nautical parlance for Starboard side to the quay).

I remember one Saturday in Glasgow when we were told by the Mate not to go ashore as Rangers were playing Celtic. Apparently the streets were turned into rivers of blood on these occasions. We were treated to some entertainment though when standing out on deck we watched a very drunk seaman returning to his tug berthed across the dock from us. He was singing, 'I belong to Glasgy' as he staggered perilously close to the quayside. He eventually reached the position of the tug whose deck was about eighteen feet below the quay. There was a long almost vertical ladder that was the sole access to the tug. We were very alarmed that this very drunken fellow was going to climb down the ladder that was clearly not secured at either top or bottom, but there was clearly nothing we could do about it. As he climbed down rung by precarious rung the ladder came off the quayside and swayed precariously outwards. We were sure that he was going to be thrown out into the dock, but the patron saint of drunken seamen was looking down on him and somehow he reached the deck of the tug. We gave him a rapturous round of applause, to which he responded with a bow and little dance. This memory has held me in good stead since that day and I have always taken particular care of gangways and their suitability.

When we had completed discharging our cargo we entered the dry dock for some repairs. It was tremendously exciting for two seventeen-year-old lads to climb down into the dry-dock and walk under the ship's keel. We watched as the propeller was removed and the tail shaft withdrawn. Several dented shipside plates were removed, rolled flat and riveted back in place. The riveting hammers made a terrific noise and we were glad when that job was finished. One thing in particular that I remember from that docking was the shipwrights calking the seams on the bridge and Monkey Island and then paying the seams with pitch much as Dad taught me to do on the old punt.

One of our tasks was cleaning all the bridge brass. It was a soulless job and to this day I cannot think of any useful purpose that it solved. We would spend hours each week polishing the sidelights that stood out in the open, exposed to the elements, where they would be green by the following day. One Saturday afternoon we were cleaning the lights when Clive knocked over the can of Brasso. It went all over the pristine wooden deck right outside the Captain's cabin. We tried desperately to clean it up but nothing would lift the huge white mark. In desperation we sought out the Bosun who luckily for us hadn't gone ashore. He introduced us to the Seaman's Prayer Book or Holystone. This was a heavy block of sandstone that, on bended knees, we pushed up and down the planks with a liberal supply of sand and water. A time-honoured tradition dating back centuries, this was a thankless task that resulted in severe backache but none the less was very effective in removing the stain. We were to become very well acquainted with holystones!!!

It was during our stay in Glasgow that we learned that one of our Captain's predilections was to have us learn and recite the articles or Rules Of The Road (the seaman's equivalent to the Highway Code). There were originally 16 rules that covered right of way, recognition lights and shapes and sound signals. Originally crisp and clear, they have since been added to and amended to by politicians and lawyers such that they have lost a lot of their original clout. We were expected to learn one article a day and would be tested on them before being granted shore leave. As it was we were so hard up on our meagre salaries that we were seldom able to afford to step foot off the ship even if we could remember them.

We left the dry-dock and went onto the loading berth before returning to Liverpool. Ellerman & Papayanni were a liner company offering regular sailings from Liverpool to the Mediterranean, advertising in shipping papers like the *Liverpool Journal of Commerce*. The *Maltasian* was advertised as calling at Gibraltar, Malta, Libya, Greece and Turkey and other ports if inducement made a stop worthwhile. We were booked to load at Swansea and Barrie before eventually going foreign.

I had to pinch myself at times to prove that this was not a dream and that I was really there aboard that ship sailing off to foreign parts to realise my childhood dreams.

Leaving Barrie we headed down the Bristol Channel. We hadn't gone far before we were in a full westerly gale blowing in from the Atlantic. The sea became very rough and by the time we were level with Lundy Island we were hove to. Clive was not a good sailor and remained in his bunk. I was more than happy and loved the savagery of the ocean. On the second morning I was tucking into a hearty breakfast of eggs bacon and griddlecake on top of curry and rice, (for some strange reason Liverpool based ships always had curry and rice on the breakfast menu) when the Chief Officer came into the saloon. He took one look at my plate and rushed outside. He never was a good sailor either.

Ellermans had a very high reputation for building fine seaworthy ships. There were many tales told in the Officers' Dining Saloon and

Lounge of heroics performed during the recent war. We Apprentices were enraptured by stories of those dreadful times when so many ships sailing in convoy were sunk by enemy submarines and huge numbers of lives were lost. Many of the officers at sea at that time had been involved in the war and would recount their experiences. At the commencement of hostilities the Ellerman combined fleet stood at 105, of which 25 were owned by Ellerman and Papayanni. Total fleet losses totalled 60, of which 19 were owned by Papayanni, an appalling 67%.

One story that particularly affected me was that of the *City of Benares.*

The story of this ill-fated ship was particularly tragic. Built in 1936 she was reported to be the most beautiful ship owned by Ellermans and widely held as among the loveliest built. At 11,081 tons she was undeniably flagship of the combined Ellerman fleets.

In 1940 she came under the direction of the Ministry of Shipping and the Government's 'Children's Overseas Evacuation Board'. On 12 of September 1940 she embarked passengers at Prince's floating landing stage before moving out to anchor in the Mersey. She sailed at 1800 hours the following day, in ballast, for Montreal with 406 persons aboard of which 209 were crew, 6 convoy staff and 191 passengers including 90 children and 10 escorts.

City of Benares was Commodore ship of a 19-ship 8-knot convoy (less than half her service speed). The convoy escorts were one destroyer and two sloops. The convoy sailed in three lines with *City of Benares* lead ship of the centre line. At 0100 on the 17th the escorting warships, having reached the extremity of their steaming range, left the convoy to continue out into the Atlantic unescorted.

At 2205 hours that night the *City of Benares* was hit by a torpedo fired from a German submarine. With the vessel sinking, the order was given to abandon ship and despite severe weather and hampered by darkness, all the lifeboats were launched within 15 minutes. Tragically several boats were swamped by waves and lost. At 2245 the *City of Benares* sank beneath the cold waters of the North Atlantic with the loss in all of 248 lives, including the Captain. Of these losses 77 were children and 5 escorts.

On September 18 the destroyer HMS *Hurricane* rescued survivors from a raft and several lifeboats, a total of 105, of whom 5 died aboard ship. Miraculously 8 days after the ship sank, one remaining lifeboat was sighted by a Sunderland aircraft who radioed for assistance before returning to drop food to the heavily overloaded lifeboat.

At 1700 hours on 25th of September the destroyer HMS *Anthony* reached the remaining 45 survivors, including 6 children, all of whom were safely landed at Greenock the following day. Following the tragic loss of the *City of Benares* the evacuation by sea policy ceased.

With the British Empire extending to most corners of the world in those postwar days most premier British shipping companies still ran a number of passenger ships within their fleets.

Even the cargo ships would have a couple of cabins set aside for passengers, and to travel by cargo ship was considered a very pleasant relaxed means of getting to some of the more remote destinations. The standard of food was thus very high on both passenger and cargo vessels. Breakfast and lunch were substantial meals but dinner usually consisted of a five-course meal with silver service. As most companies expected their officers to dine with the passengers, etiquette and table manners were important. As apprentices we sat at one of the junior officers' tables and were quickly shown the niceties of decorum required in the Officers' Dining Saloon.

It took us three days to get around Lands End. The Bay of Biscay was calm in comparison to what we had just experienced, but as we sailed down the west coast of Portugal the weather began to get warmer and by the time we passed Lisbon we were into Tropical Kit. Clive and I were both very excited on reaching Casablanca, our first foreign port. The ship dropped anchor off the port, and a tug brought out a barge and labour to discharge our cargo. I was mesmerised by the different smells, which came offshore on the breeze. This was Morocco, and looking at the silhouette of the town I could make out minarets and mosques and white painted houses. This was the stuff that every schoolboy's dreams are made of.

We stopped briefly at Gibraltar to discharge cargo and take on bunkers and then headed into the Mediterranean for Malta where a truly unique spectacle awaited us. As we entered Grand Harbour we were amazed to see what appeared to be half the Royal Navy present. The Aircraft Carrier *Ark Royal* and the Cruiser *Lion* were there with the Mediterranean Fleet and also the Carrier *Eagle* with her escort group, on their way home from the Far East. That night the Navy lit up the town. I shall never forget looking down Straight Street (better known as The Gut), which was reputed to have a bar on every step. There was just a seething mass of blue and white navy uniforms. Remarkably there were very few incidents, mainly due I guess to the heavy presence of military police. Compared with today's football crowds they were little angels.

We continued our Mediterranean cruise calling at Tripoli and several Greek ports before arriving at our last discharging port at Istanbul. Sitting either side of the Bosphorus, this enchanting city was full of mystique and romance. Besides dozens of ferries threading their way across, there was a constant procession of ships of all types passing up and down this busy waterway leading to the Black Sea. It is quite strange to have such a busy and politically important international highway running through the middle of a city. We did manage to get ashore and visited the Blue Mosque and the church of Santa Sofia. One thing that amazed me was that all the Turkish men had moustaches. It's strange how some thoughts remain in one's mind.

Return cargoes from the Mediterranean would usually be fruit or other foodstuffs but this trip we were sent back to Tripoli to load army vehicles where the British army was preparing to pull out of Libya. We loaded huge tank transporters in the centre of the hold, Bedford trucks around the sides and Land Rovers to fill in the gaps. Once the loading was complete the hold was floored over with timber and old hatch boards so that we could top up with oranges from Southern Spain. Whilst we were loading in Malaga Clive and I were intrigued to see men on the quayside selling little birds in tiny wooden cages. We were shocked when we realised that these were wild finches and despite the pecuniary state of our finances we bought two of the pretty little birds so that we could immediately release them. The oranges had to be loaded with tunnels between the cases to allow air to circulate. Our job was to ensure that the tunnels were made correctly and we worked almost continuously in the hold. The air heavy with citric gases caused painful sore throats and we were never so glad as to see the end of the load. All the Papayanni ships were fitted with big extractor fans in ventilators along the deck specifically for the fruit trade. The smell of the fruit on deck would normally have been quite pleasant but for us two, having spent 18 hours a day for four days amongst the oranges, we could happily have done without it.

The shippers had put several cases of oranges onboard as a thank you to the officers. When we reached Liverpool where we were sent on leave, the Chief Officer told us to each take a case of oranges home. These were the nicest oranges I have ever tasted. It wasn't until some years later that I discovered that we had mistakenly taken the special oranges intended for the Captain's table.

I arrived home just in time for Christmas and had a wonderful leave regaling my family and friends with stories of all the wonderful places that I had visited. The end of my leave came all to soon and I was instructed to join my next ship, the SS *Anglian* in Liverpool bound for the South of France and Italy.

My mother kept all my letters and the following is an extract from one of them dated 21 January 1960.

> We arrived here (Savona Italy) on Thursday morning after a two hour run across from Genoa. We are at anchor in the harbour waiting for a

> berth. The French and Italian Riviera is very beautiful. As we came across the Gulf of Genoa dawn was just breaking and the beautiful panorama, which opened as the curtain was raised, made us literally gasp for breath. As the sun rose in a huge ball of fire over the snow capped mountains the sky was a glorious mass of colour. The high white temple spires of the Alps slowly descended to green valleys and hills. The sea was a deep cobalt blue flecked with little white topped waves and fringed by golden sandy bays and rocky headlands. The guidebooks say that this is some of the most beautiful scenery in the world and by golly they were right there. We have already loaded five hundred tons of pears, tomatoes and starch in Marseilles and Genoa and we have come here to load one thousand tons of rice for Manchester and so it looks as if we will be going up the canal this time.

The little *Anglian* was well suited to that run as she had an additional tween deck called the orlop deck that gave more flexibility in loading cargo. The ship would both discharge and load at each port making the job of the Chief Officer a nightmare. By the time we had completed discharging at Naples our tween decks were more than half full and we were sent up to Livorno to load marble. The heavy stone had to be loaded low down in the ship for stability. When we sailed from Livorno it was out into a raging storm. The Gulf of Lions can produce some very bad weather.

When I had joined my first ship in Liverpool I had been disgusted at the state of their public transport. The seats on the dockside buses were so dirty that one's clothes would be ruined if you sat down. The Liverpool docker would go to work in the same clothes day in day out. In comparison the continental dockers would arrive dressed in clean clothes and then change into working clothes that, frequently patched, would again be freshly washed and ironed. And to think that we had the gall to call the French dirty frogs!

It was whilst I was on the *Anglian* that I bought my very first pair of jeans. Dad had never allowed us kids to wear jeans, which he likened to workman's overalls. I remember buying them for ten shillings from a shop in West India Dock Road, in the East End of London. That night we had sailed from the Thames and as we went out into the Estuary there was a stiff wind blowing spray across the foredeck. Whilst battening down the hatches we got very wet and by the time I reached my cabin my lovely new jeans had shrunk so much that Clive had to get scissors to cut them off my legs. I guess that was my first lesson in why not to buy cheap clothes.

I enjoyed the Italian run but was very excited when told at the end of the trip that our next one was to South West Africa.

We left the cold British winter behind and were soon into the tropics. It was then that I saw my first flying fish skimming across the surface of the sea, a sight that has thrilled me ever since. There were schools of dolphins frolicking around the ship and riding the bow wave. The ship had been chartered to another branch of the Ellerman Empire to inaugurate a new scheduled run to Lobito and Walvis Bay. We carried general cargo out and a full cargo of tinned pilchards and bagged fishmeal home. Sitting on the edge of the Kalahari Dessert, Walvis Bay relies solely on the fishing industry for its existence. The sea along this coast produced a rich harvest and while we were loading in the port we watched the fishing trawlers coming in so heavily laden with pilchards that they were in serious danger of sinking.

One morning we were to witness a horrific accident. I was standing on deck wondering at the fact that the majority of dockside cranes around the world were built in Bath England by Stothert & Pit. The crane was mounted on a platform supported by four legs some thirty feet tall and surrounded on three sides by a hand rail at waist height. An African guy, whose job it was to lubricate the gearing of the cranes, was walking around the platform with the oilcan in his hand. He was walking backwards as the counter weight traversed towards him. The clearance between the weight and the handrail was no more than two to three inches. Suddenly the workman came up against the handrail with the weight still coming towards him. People standing on the quayside saw what was happening and shouted to the crane driver. By the time the driver knew that anything was wrong, the poor guy was dead. I was most impressed that it was that same crane driver who went up in a basket, lifted by another crane, to collect up the remains. Even the Doctor who attended was sick at the sight of this tragic accident. It certainly had a very significant affect on me a seventeen-year-old lad.

Ships are very dangerous places and only too often work-related accidents happen. Some years later I was standing by the side of a hatch watching cargo being discharged when a similar accident occurred. A Greaser was oiling the winch beside me. He climbed up onto the hatch coming to save time getting to the other side. I told him that his action was stupid and dangerous when something caught my eye. The winch started up and the Greaser fell backwards down into the hold some forty feet down. The hold was loaded with steel roof trusses for the army but fortunately for the Greaser the forward twenty feet was loaded with foam rubber mattresses. Landing on this soft base he got up, climbed up out of the hatch and carried on working as if nothing had happened. Some people I guess are just born lucky, unlike the African fellow.

Many accidents happen as a result of carelessness. I nearly lost the sight in one eye when a slither of steel imbedded itself in my right eye. I had been painting around the lower bridge and found a small patch of rust. As I was in a hurry to get finished and go ashore I didn't go to the store for goggles but just chipped at the spot with a chipping hammer. Suddenly a piece of steel flew up and hit me in the eye. The Chief Steward washed out my eye with saline solution but when about a week later the Chief Officer noticed that I was still squinting he sent me ashore to the doctor in Famagusta, Cyprus. The doc immediately referred me to an eye specialist who operated to remove the foreign object. He told me that if it had remained for another day it could have penetrated the cornea and I would have lost my sight. Fifty years later, the scar still remains. I guess I owe that Greek doctor a great deal of gratitude.

My childhood holidays on the Mudeford Sandbank at the bottom of Christchurch harbour had given me a good understanding of tidal cycles. The marshes at the edge of the harbour were criss-crossed by creeks, which were all linked together and ultimately drained, into the larger Lime Kiln Creek that then emptied into the harbour. At high water especially at springs there was plenty of water to navigate my punt. The high spring tides occurred fortnightly and would be in the late morning. Because of our position near to the Isle of Wight the water ebbing down the English Channel would push up into the Solent and Christchurch bay. This would create a stand or second high about an hour after the first high. For a young boy playing at smugglers and pirates this was truly heaven-sent. People walking along the edge of the harbour would suddenly be confronted by the creek. Their options were to try wading the creek or retrace their tracks and take the road running under the hillside of Hengistbury Head. The third option was to be ferried across the creek by me in my punt. I had been taught never to ask for money but usually the grateful travellers would reward me for my kindness. I remember one Bank Holiday weekend, with the sky heavy with threatening thunderstorms, making thirty shillings, which was like a king's ransom to me.

When I was thirteen I was introduced by a friend to Christchurch Sailing Club. My horizons were opened and I started crewing on yachts of all sizes. There was always a shortage of crew and I learned quickly the skills and boat-craft needed to be of use. I was soon introduced to the thrills and spills of dinghy racing. There is nothing to my mind more exhilarating than to be out on the trapeze wire on a fast planning dinghy as it skims across the surface of the water.

My parents bought me a twelve-foot Firefly dinghy for my sixteenth birthday and I was in my element sailing this around the harbour. When

I was on leave during the summer months I would wake to the dawn chorus and stealthily leave the house to cycle the half mile to the Sailing Club. It would take me only ten minutes to get the dinghy out of the shed and rigged. Sailing down the river to the harbour as the sun came up over the horizon was pure magic to me. There would not be another person on the water that I would share with the swans and ducks. Families of moorhen and coots would forage for food in the river whilst in the harbour there would be sheldrake and widgeon that would dive as I approached, only to surface several yards away. By the time I returned home my family were just getting up and I was ready for one of Mum's cooked breakfasts.

I stayed on the *Anglian* for over a year and was very happy there, but my next ship was quite different. By now Clive had left (he couldn't stand the terrible seasickness that he suffered every time the weather turned nasty) and another apprentice joined me. There was never that same fraternal bond that developed from our starting off together on our new career. On the *Patrician* I did make a good friend however in Jimmy, our Fifth Engineer, who had done his apprenticeship as a motor mechanic. Jimmy had never been abroad before and on his first trip as we sailed down the Portuguese coast and the weather began to get warm he would take no heed of our warnings and became seriously sunburnt. I remember the Chief Engineer on that ship having a budgie in his cabin and Jimmy trying to teach it rude words, but all it would say was 'sun's over the yardarm lads'. Perhaps Jimmy should have listened to him. Some four or five days later we were in Malta and having a free afternoon decided to go swimming. Malta in those days boasted several quiet little sandy bays before the package holiday hotels invaded the Island. Whilst we frolicked in the warm water I suddenly noticed that Jimmy appeared to be wearing a shirt. It was in fact his top layer of skin that had come away. Although unsightly it didn't cause him any pain and he quickly recovered, but from then on would always be careful of the sun.

The *Patrician* was not a happy ship and at one stage I wrote home to my parents saying that I wanted to give up the sea and have a change of career. Fortunately Dad wrote to Captain Bates our Superintendent and I was posted to the *City of Leeds*. This was a fairly new ship and had like the *Anglian* been chartered out to inaugurate a new service. We loaded in London and the near Continent for a direct service to Sarawak and North Borneo. Cargo previously had been transhipped via Singapore and then again transferred into barges to get to the hinterland. The Company Agent in Singapore was a keen yachtsman and spent his summer holidays exploring the Ragang River delta. It was on one of these trips that he discovered a deep-water channel running some eighty miles inland to the town of Sibu. Within a month of his discovery the first of our ships sailed from London offering the shippers direct service to Kuching and Sibu. We also called at such lovely little port as Jesselton, Sandakan and Tawao. It was an incredible voyage and reawoke in me my thirst for travelling to remote places. We had a great Captain who showed a keen interest in the training of us Apprentices and most of my time on passage was spent on the bridge learning the mysteries of spherical trigonometry and other aspects of navigation. It was the general practice for Apprentices to take the wheel when entering and leaving port. This trip gave me the chance of not only steering through the Egyptian desert as we ran through the Suez Canal but way up into the jungle rivers of Borneo.

We had been away for some four months and as we sailed up the English Channel I had my first experience of *'The Channels'* (strong emotional nostalgia felt by British travellers about to sight the White Cliffs of Dover after lengthy journeys). Standing on deck as we came up channel, I could see numerous large passenger ships heading in both directions. Ships sailing from London and Southampton answered the need for British people going to and fro between the old Empire and home. There were Union Castle to South and East Africa; Shaw Saville and NZSC to New Zealand; Royal Mail and PSNC to South America. P&O and Orient Line to The Far East; BI and Ellermans to South and East Africa and of course Cunard to the USA, to name but a few. There were no traffic separation schemes in those days and passage through the Dover Straights was extremely hazardous in clear weather let alone in fog.

Much to the relief of my parents, by the time I returned home, I was once again totally committed to a life at sea. I arrived home just before Christmas and was greeted by my mother saying 'No thanks we don't want to buy anything,' before she closed the door on me. She hadn't recognised me as I was darkly tanned and sported a full beard. On Christmas Eve I received a telephone call from Captain Bates who said that he had received such a good report of me from my Captain that he was offering me promotion to Third Officer. As I had only just started the fourth year of my apprenticeship this was a great surprise to me and was the best Christmas present I could have asked for. I was to report to his office before joining the MV *Malatian* in Liverpool on New Year's Eve. Arriving at the office wearing my uniform with the single gold band on my sleeve I waited outside the Super's office. I was surprised when a chap came out and asked if I was joining the *Malatian*. On my replying yes he wished me the best of luck adding, 'You will need it. The Old Man is a bastard. He has sacked six third mates in six months.'

Somewhat concerned I entered Captain Bates' office. He congratulated me on my promotion and wished me well and before dismissing me said with a wry smile 'Captain Pedley is expecting you.' It was good to be sailing again with this man who had been so instrumental with the launching of my career. I continued to learn much from him and remained on the *Malatian* until I had completed my qualifying time for my Second Mate's certificate.

We were running on a monthly service to North Africa from Liverpool, picking up whatever cargo was available on the return voyage. On one trip we had just passed through the Straights of Gibraltar outward bound when we heard the devastating news that the *Patrician* had been sunk off of Receffi at the entrance to the Straights. This must have happened within a couple of hours of us passing the spot. The accident occurred in thick fog, the *Patrician* having just left Gib on her way home. She had collided with an American ship, like us inbound through the Straights. My thoughts immediately went out to all my friends on board, especially Jimmy. We learnt later that day that the Captain, Chief Officer and Radio Officer were missing but the remainder of the crew were accounted for, including the Chief Engineer's budgie. Jimmy came down to stay at Christchurch later and regaled me with the grim story of how he had been rescued from the water by a lifeboat from the American vessel. He never went back to sea again. Since that dreadful day I have always said a little prayer when passing that spot.

2

THE LURE OF THE ORIENT

I always think that the magic of the East starts at Suez. Once through the Canal and into the heat of the Red Sea the stage is set and the wonders unfold. It wasn't long after finishing my indentures before I was back on the Borneo run. This time it was as Third Officer aboard the old Ionian renamed the *City of Durham*. Although she was the sister ship to the *Patrician* this was a very happy ship.

After earlier crewing problems the Company had decided to man her with Somali ratings. We were somewhat apprehensive at first but these chaps proved themselves good seamen and very hard workers. Unlike the London crew they were sober and well behaved. The Bosun was King of the Foc'sle and ruled his crew with a rod of iron. Of an evening you would find all off-watch personnel sitting on one of the after hatches, grouped around the Bosun learning English. Their homeport was Swansea where they had entered the country having first served an apprenticeship on dhows before being schooled by the Royal Navy in Aden to achieve Able Seaman status. At the end of each voyage the Bosun would advise the Mate of any staff he wanted to get rid of and would present the discharge books of replacements that he recommended. In this way he maintained his authority and we were very pleased with the results.

Having completed my indentured time on the *Malatian,* back in August of that year I had a couple of weeks spare before I was due to commence studying for my Second Mate's Certificate at Warsash. Hearing that the Company were short staffed in Liverpool, I offered my services. Completion of my indentured time would mean coming off pay and I would have to be self-sufficient until I signed on aboard my next ship. A couple of extra weeks pay would come in very useful, besides it would give me the opportunity to meet up with old girl friends and visit the Cavern where the Beatles were then performing.

Before finally leaving Liverpool I was again called in to see the Superintendent. Thinking that I was in for a bollocking, imagine my surprise when Captain Bates thanked me for helping them out of a spot and said that in view of my record he was awarding me two months additional pay for studying. This proved an absolute godsend and set me up well. By Christmas I had completed my studies and with a brand new Certificate, presented myself to the Company for sea service once again.

That trip on the old Ionian was pure magic to me. Although an old ship her steam turbine propulsion gave her a top speed of around fifteen knots, but for most of her life on the Mediterranean service she had been run at an economical speed of eleven knots. It was good to feel the ship responding to that power which the builders had given her. Fifteen knots for a ship of less than four thousand tons was unusual and it felt good to be overtaking other vessels for a change.

As we approached the coast of Ceylon (now Srilanka) I could smell the cooking fires some thirty miles offshore. The lovely smell of wood burning conjured up images of the local people clustered in their villages with their fishing boats pulled up on the shore.

We reached Singapore, where for me the Orient really begins, and I remember the wishy-washy women clambering aboard to do our dhobi for a bar of soap or a couple of pennies. We were joined there by the senior Director from our Agents, who was coming with us to Kuching for a shippers' party. I remember him being very disappointed with the ship as she was dated and the decks black from the soot from the boilers that had been struggling to give us the recommended speed. I volunteered to get the party venue tidied up and the Mate gave me unlimited overtime for the crew that he put at my disposal.

From Singapore to Kuching was only a couple of days' passage but with half an hour to go I invited the Director to come up on deck to see the product of our labours. To say that he was gob-smacked was an understatement. On the deck abaft the bridge the paintwork had all been sooggied, new canvas awnings stretched across the awning spars, new hatch tarpaulins stretched without a crease across the cargo hatch, an assortment of flags covered the lifeboat winches, and the decks had been holystoned to a sun bleached white. Tables were set with white linen and the catering staff in freshly laundered uniforms were carrying trays of food and drink up from below. The whole space was lit with coloured fairy lights.

He was very impressed and with a feeling of achievement I met our first guests, the Governor of Sarawak and North Borneo and his lady, whom I escorted up to be received by the Captain and the Director. The party was such a success that instead of winding up at nine o'clock it continued until well after midnight, The Governor and his Lady being the last to leave.

The following day we commenced discharging our cargo. One of the main reasons why our ship had been selected for this run was her ability to handle heavy cargo coupled with her size. She was only just over 3,000 tons gross, which enabled her to reach some of the smaller inland ports, yet she had the gear to lift weights of up to 40 tons. For normal discharge two derricks would be used, one plumbing the hold and one over the side. The two runners would be connected to form a union purchase and slings would be swung up out of the hold and swayed outboard to either a barge or the quayside. These derricks could also be rigged as single swinging derricks. With heavy purchase blocks fitted they could lift up to ten tons. For loads up to forty tons we had two jumbo or heavy lift derricks, one forward and one aft. These would normally be housed in the fully erect position stowed hard back against the mast. These had now to be rigged with the huge purchase blocks and steam guys to control the swing. In total five steam winches were used to operate the jumbo. This operation was totally new to our Somali crew and in fact the only person on board with experience to handle this gear was Mr Mac the First Mate.

Mac was one of life's characters. Born in Stornaway in the Outer Hebrides he attended a small croft school that he left at fifteen with a rudimentary education. By the time he was eighteen he owned his own fishing boat. He joined the merchant navy at the outbreak of war and by twenty-five was quartermaster on the *Queen Mary*. Deciding that he wanted to be a captain he studied and by his thirty-fifth birthday had obtained his master's certificate. Working his way up from the Foc's'le he was an extremely good seaman and his lovely soft Hebridean brogue gave him a quiet air of authority. We spent the morning rigging and operating the big derricks until Mac was happy and confident in the crew's ability to handle them. Watching him directing operations with just his hands, arms and a whistle was pure genius. I learned so much from that man.

Many heavy pieces of cargo were stowed in the holds, together with the more general cargo, but the particularly large pieces were stowed on deck. The largest was a big launch of about sixty feet in length that stowed across number two hatch hung out over the ship's side. With the clanking and hissing of the steam winches this huge boat was lifted from its cradle and slowly swung out over the side. Such a weight suspended outboard could have an alarming effect on stability and Mac had been at pains all morning to ensure that all of our water tanks were both full and pressed up. Even so the ship listed heavily as the weight was slowly swung outboard. It was amazing that once in the water it looked so much smaller than it had looked sitting on deck.

I don't think that I could ever reach Mac's standard but I certainly learned a tremendous amount from our time together. The Director told us that the freight on the heavy lifts alone had paid for the outward trip. If that was so then we must have had an extremely profitable voyage.

Kuching was a beautiful town with most of the buildings in the colonial style, the most significant being the residence of the White Raja with its white painted walls and thatched roof. Although Kuching was the capital it was a relatively small town in those days and didn't gain city status until 1988. With the river meandering through park-like areas of neatly tended lawns and beautiful trees dotted around, it was so English that it reminded me of Stratford upon Avon.

The South China Sea has always been a hunting ground for pirates, who were particularly active in Victorian times when trade was rapidly expanding. The adventurer James Brooke, an opportunist of somewhat dubious character himself, in 1838 offered his services and that of his ship, *The Royalist*, to the Sultan of Brunei in quelling a Dayak uprising, *The Royalist* being a heavily armed merchant vessel with a well disciplined crew. In return for achieving a peaceful settlement he was granted the title of Rajah of Sarawak; allbeit some reports say that this was given under duress. Brooke began to establish and cement his rule over Sarawak, reforming the administration, codifying laws and fighting piracy. His achievement was recognised by the British Government and during a visit to England in 1847 he was given the Freedom of the City of London, appointed Governor, Commander-in-chief of Labuan, and British consul-general in Borneo. He was also created a KCB.

Little did they know at that time how the discovery of oil in Brunei would so dramatically affect the fortunes of the Sultan. Such knowledge could have significantly changed the political map of the area. His legacy remained however until Sarawak and North Borneo gained their independence from Britain and became part of the Federation of Malaysia in 1963.

Whilst our ship was at Singapore The Chief Engineer, Fourth Engineer and I had purchased a canoe that we wanted to use for exploring some of the rivers. It was not much more than a native dug-out and very unstable. We fitted an outrigger to one side and with a lot of practice became quite adept at handling our little boat. Whenever we managed to get time off we would paddle off up the creeks, totally absorbed with the wild life and scenery. The banks were heavily covered with mangroves that liked their roots totally immersed in water.

One day whilst we were at Sibu we went off on one of our exploratory missions and discovered a Dayak village. The Dayaks are native to Borneo and live in longhouses built on stilts up above the ground. As we paddled by, the children all came running down to see this strange sight. Eager to take some photos I persuaded the other two to take me to the bank where some big logs had been pulled half out of the water. Hopping out of the canoe, camera slung around my neck, I discovered to my horror that the log I had chosen to jump onto wasn't grounded and started to rotate. I must have given quite a comedy act as I tried desperately to get my balance. The other two had backed out into midstream leaving me to negotiate my rolling log. The children who had all run off as I had approached soon plucked up courage to come closer to see this funny man dancing on logs.

The weather in Borneo is extremely changeable and without warning the heavens opened in a deluge of rain. Not wanting my camera to get wet I ran up to shelter under the longhouse. An old man hung out of the doorway and beckoned to me to come up. The other two seeing my good fortune and not wanting to miss out hurriedly came ashore.

The Dayaks were amazingly hospitable and we sat around with the men in a circle whilst the women and children stood at one end of the hut. With the aid of one young lad, who spoke quite good English, acting as interpreter we managed to converse with them. They wanted to know where we had come from in our funny little boat and where we were going. We had a case of beer in the canoe that we offered and was much appreciated. They were all dressed the same in just a sarong that was a colourful skirt wrapped around the waist. The women were quite unabashed at being naked above the waist.

It must have been a couple of hours that we stayed there amongst these lovely friendly people. It was hard to believe that only a couple of generations earlier these people could have been headhunters. As we prepared to depart they all gathered together for a photograph but insisted in putting on their best clothes which turned out to be western shirts and trousers for the men and dresses for the women. This was such a disappointment after seeing them in their natural colourful simplistic innocence in their sarongs.

We left them promising to return on our next trip. In fact we did just that, some four months later and were astounded to discover that they had got news of our ship's return and had prepared a banquet for us. There was amazing food and a locally made alcohol that blew your head off but for diplomacy had to be drunk. They were truly amazing people. Years later when my eldest daughter, a medical student in London, announced that she was going to Borneo as part of her training, I asked 'Why on earth go to Borneo?' Her reply was 'Daddy, when we were kids, you filled us with such wonderful stories of your exploits there that I just had to go see for myself.' I am pleased to say that she wasn't disappointed.

Sibu had a colourful outdoor food market consisting of several small kitchens with tables and chairs all covered in colourful awnings. The food was magnificent, ranging from the horrifically expensive local bird's nest soup to a local dish of fish stew that was served in a metal dish called a steamboat. The dish resembled a castle with a moat. The castle held hot charcoal whilst the moat contained the delicious fish stew. The only problem was that just about everything went into the stew and it was a bit unnerving to eat a mouthful of fish eyes.

Once we had completed our discharge at all the small ports around the coast we were sent to another part of the Rajang Delta called Tanjong Mani to load timber for our homeward cargo. There were a number of large vessels anchored there and it was fascinating watching the small local wooden vessels chugging back and forth like ants supplying timber to feed the demands of the Western world. We loaded thousands of tons of sawn timber into the holds and once they were full we lifted huge logs onto the deck. There were special securing devices and wires with quick release mechanisms fitted in case the deck cargo had to be jettisoned in an emergency. The whole place was a hive of activity and little did we realise at that time how we were adding to the tragedy that was to become the deforestation of Borneo and the destruction of the rain forests. No doubt we were being watched by the orangutans whose ancestors had occupied these forests for thousands of years.

I remained on the *City of Durham* for two trips. It was during the second that I made a decision to change companies. We were alongside in Singapore and the Second Mate pointed out the ship berthed ahead of us and told me that that was the company I should join if I wanted to see more of The East. She was the *Bulimba* belonging to British India Steam Navigation Company, or BI as they were known.

I decided to go ship visiting and walked along the quay. On asking to see the Duty Officer, the Quartermaster, or I should say sukunni, after making a telephone call, showed me to the Second Mate's cabin. I explained my interest and was warmly received. His cabin was enormous and sumptuous in comparison to my cabin. He had a settee, armchair coffee table, large desk and chair and an icebox for chilled beer. The cabin had its own bathroom and altogether made our accommodation look rather squalid. All of the accommodation was air-conditioned and I quickly realised that this was the lifestyle I would like to live.

Of course the other man's grass is always greener and I did not appreciate that this ship was ultra modern by the BI general standard. In fact I later read in Lloyds List that BI were considered to be experts at running out of date shipping. However the thought of India drew me on and I tendered my letter of resignation to Papayannis and applied to BI for a post as Third Mate.

After we left Singapore we called at Port Swetnam and Penang, which in those days was a sleepy little island far removed from the tourist destination of today. Then we were instructed to call at the little island of Gan in the Maldives. Gan was a tiny corral atoll and was the host to the RAF on one of the loneliest postings in the forces. We were having engine problems with the boilers using an inordinate amount of water. To augment our fresh water supply (not being able in those days to make our own) we dodged the rainstorms prevalent in the Indian Ocean at that time of year. By dodging I mean attempting to catch as much rainfall as possible. With hoses rigged to the scupper pipes leading down from the bridge and boat decks, and connected to the filling pipes we were able to gather enough water to keep the boilers going. The offset of this strange course across the ocean was that as we approached the Island they were unable to detect our ship on radar and we had entered the lagoon before the RAF knew we were there. They certainly were glad to see us and gave the Officers a wonderful party ashore. I remember trying to nick, as a souvenir, a photograph of Jayne Mansfield from the Mess, but its absence was noted before our departure and a raiding party relieved us of our spoils. It was certainly a most memorable call.

By the time we reached Aden the boilers needed some serious TLC and technicians were flown out from the UK to undertake repairs. It seems that the flogging that the poor old boilers had taken was too much for them, and the ship was sold at the end of that voyage. It was with happy memories that I left her in the Royal Docks in London where she looked quite small amongst the huge passenger liners in the docks, but she had done us proud.

I think I inherited my fascination for the East from my mother. My grandfather was an Officer in the British Army stationed in Jhansi, a small town in Uttar Pradesh, India, when Mum was born in 1914. She remembered very little about India and it was my grandmother who really awakened my interest with stories of the North West Frontier and the Khyber Pass. Those were the days of the British Raj and were pure magic to the ears of a young boy. I had always longed to see this strange country, so different from the suburban England where I had been raised.

BI deployed part of their fleet on trade from the UK to East Africa and the Far East referred to as the 'Home Line' but their major interest was in trades that never reached Western Europe. These ships were on 'Eastern Service' and Officers serving on them were deployed for two and a half years without being granted leave.

The Sixties were certainly a period of great change and little did I realise how much would change at home during the next two and a half years. Lord Beeching was making shattering changes to the railways and steam trains would be replaced by diesel or electric, motorways would be built all over the country, BP would discover oil in the North Sea, and Mary Quant was to liberate ladies' legs, to say nothing of the introduction of colour television and England winning the World Cup.

Having been accepted by BI, I was instructed to meet a party at Waterloo Station in readiness to join the *Devonia* in Genoa as a supernumery for passage to India. I had received another list of uniform but this one was far larger than the one I had from Ellermans five years earlier. I had been given a load of uniforms by a dear old lady from Christchurch Sailing Club. Mrs Savage, bless her, had always shown an interest in us youngsters and was delighted to give me the uniforms that her son had worn in the Royal Navy. Because BI had many passenger ships, we were required to have various types of dress uniforms for evening wear. During the war he had been Flag Lieutenant to Lord Mountbatten, seeing service in the Indian theatre of the war. His uniforms had been methodically stored and did me many years' service. My full sea-going kit now filled two sea chests.

Another interesting piece of my kit was a little book entitled *'Malim Sahib's Hindustani'*. As it said on the front cover, this book was 'for ship's officers who wish to acquire a working knowledge of low Hindustani spoken by native crews, servants and longshoremen generally'. This little book was to be of great value to me and richly augmented the few words of Hindustani that my grandmother had taught me all those years before.

The *Devonia* of 11,275 tons had been built as the *Devonshire* and equipped as a troop ship for Ben Line. She was sister ship to BI's *Dunera.* Although the Jumbo Jet was yet to have its devastating effect on world travel, with the transfer of independence to many parts of the British Empire, by 1965 the need for troop ships had been greatly reduced. BI had come up with an innovative idea for utilising these redundant troopers and acquired the *Devonshire* they reconstructing both ships for School Cruising, an idea that was to prove highly popular and profitable. The troop decks were converted into dormitories and classrooms to accommodate 830 students, with cabin berths for 190 teachers and education officials.

On gathering at Waterloo our party embarked on our journey by train and boat train to Italy. Once across channel we remained on the same train through France and Switzerland and down into Italy, only changing at Milan for our last leg down to Genoa. Our carriage consisted of a day coach plus a sleeping coach that the attendant would make up ready for us each evening. Meals were served on the train and it was all very much like travelling on the Orient Express. There was opulence about the journey that made it very memorable. The early part of the journey through Northern France was rather boring but as we got deeper into France the scenery became more interesting and reached a dramatic pinnacle as we wound our way through the Alps and into Switzerland with the white gleaming mountain peaks and azure blue lakes. This was the right way to travel with class and style, much better than it would become later with air travel. By the time we reached Genoa I felt as if I had been on holiday. We arrived on the quayside just as the ship was docking. She had just completed a two-week cruise for German Youth Clubs that had spanned Christmas and New Year. There appeared to be twice as many women as men and most of the Officers as they escorted the passengers to the gangway seemed glad of the rest that a passage to India offered!

Taking advantage of the lull in School Cruises in the winter months *Dunera* had been taken out of commission whilst the *Devonia*, with both crews aboard, made passage to India to pick up fresh Indian crews. There was however a demand for winter cruises of this kind, well before the package holidays offering winter sun appeared, and we were to pick up a number of first class cabin passengers before departing from the Mediterranean. I was one of a number of supernumerary officers onboard destined to join ships in Pakistan and India, and our job would be to assist the Purser in looking after the passengers and arranging their entertainment. During my last leave I had taken ballroom dancing lessons. It had all started as a bit of a joke but was to be very useful when we young officers were expected to dance with the single lady passengers. I think the average age of the passengers on that cruise was sixty-five!

After a brief call at Malta we transited the Suez Canal whilst our passengers went off to visit the Pyramids, and we entered the Red Sea. I quickly found out that life on a passenger ship was very different to that of a cargo ship. Once the sun went down we were not permitted to wear shorts and short-sleeved shirts. We were expected instead to wear number 10 uniform. This consisted of long white trousers and a long tunic jacket buttoning right up to the neck. Heavily starched by the ships onboard laundry it felt rather like wearing a straight jacket. At least not needing to wear anything under the jacket gave us a little more freedom than full mess kit that was a short jacket over shirt and tie, plus of course long trousers, which was required for more formal occasions. Because of her age the ship had no air conditioning and after an evening spent escorting elderly passengers around the dance floor, one would feel utterly exhausted. I think I lost quite a few pounds in weight during the voyage. One benefit however was that I never had to buy drinks as the dear old ladies always made sure that we were kept well supplied. I was also in charge of the sweep for the day's run, which again guaranteed a number of free drinks behind the bar.

On reaching Karachi I left the cruise and joined the *Chyebassa*, a general cargo ship running between the Persian Gulf and Japan with many stops in between. She was on her way to the Gulf, an area that I came to know very well over the next two and a half years. Ports like Muscat, Dubai and Abu Dhabi were just anchorages in those days with cargo being ferried to and from the ship by barges. There was always conflict between Iraq and Iran and we would often hear shooting as we sailed up and down the Shatt al Arab River. In those days nobody at home had ever heard of the waterway or ports like Basra and Koramshar. The river and the people living on its banks fascinated me. It was as if time had stood still since biblical times, the houses, people's dress and their boats never having changed.

I had only been on the ship a few weeks when I discovered a sailing dinghy on board. The ship had picked it up adrift on the ocean one day and the boatswain, or Serang as he was called with an Indian crew, used it as a painting punt. It was absolutely covered in several inches of crusted paint. With the Chief Officer's permission I started to strip it down to bare wood. By the time we reached Bombay on our return journey to Japan she looked in pretty good condition. Bombay being our homeport we were visited by the Superintendent, who was shown the boat by the Captain. To my delight he said that he would authorise a set of sails to be supplied in Hong Kong although 'no fancy nylon stuff mind you, just cotton' were his orders. As it happened the sail maker said that cotton would cost more than double the price of Terylene and I got two suits of sails for the price of one. That little sailing boat, about sixteen feet long, half decked and with iron centreplate, gave us all a lot of fun on that ship.

As there was little to go ashore for in most of the Gulf Ports in those days we had to make or own entertainment. The ship had been built to carry up to twelve passengers and in addition to the Officers' lounge had a passenger lounge situated under the bridge. As we seldom carried passengers on that run the Captain allowed us to lay out a huge Scalectrix track in the forward lounge. Kits could be bought ashore in Japan and sometimes in Kuwait to make up our own racing cars. We would spend hours racing our little cars around that track. I had always wanted a Scalectrix set and was delighted to be given one by my colleagues and shipmates on my retirement. I have great fun now playing with it with my son and recalling those times on the old *Chyebassa*.

I was totally captivated by Bombay that was everything and more than my grandmother had told me. India never changes, it just adapts to the times. Looking at the houses and way of life in India one sees that little really has changed in thousands of years. For example take the city of Varanasi, or Benares, which was reported to have been an ancient city when visited by Buda in 500 BC. The vibrancy of the colourful dresses mixed with the multitudes of people is something that only India possesses. There is something about the Hindu people that is so relaxed and uninhibited. Because of their belief and acceptance in their caste system they seem to accept their situation in life without the avarice and greed of the western world. This results in an open and honest willingness to share their hospitality and friendship, even though most have so little themselves.

There are so many things that at first sight I would have liked to have changed in India but on closer evaluation I realise that India is India and will never change. I don't know if one loves to hate India or hates to love it. Whatever the way, like my grandmother I will never get India out of my system.

Bombay was a central port for BI and there were always a number of our ships there at any one time. As one looked across the docks the familiar black funnel with two white bands was evident everywhere. There were Eastern Service cargo ships on the Japan run and others trading to Australia, There were Home line ships coming out from the UK. But what really fascinated me were the Eastern Service passenger ships. The K class *Kampala* and *Karanja* were sizeable ships of ten thousand tons running from here to East Africa and Durban. They were certified to carry 2,441 deck passengers in addition to 240 first and second class. Then there were the little Gulf Ds *Dumra* and *Dwarka* operating a bus stop service to the Gulf ports, turning around at Basra. Also there were the *Santhia* and *Sirdana* who would fill in as required. These were trades that BI had established back in Victorian times and were still in great demand. The ships carried deck passengers who would board with their bedding rolls and lay claim to a few feet of deck space to put their bundles which in many cases contained all their worldly possessions. The Ds at under 5,000 tons carried an amazing 1,537 deck passengers. There were also cabins for first class passengers and scrutiny of the passenger list could frequently reveal Sheiks and members of aristocratic Arabic families such as the ruler of Bahrain.

I just loved the hustle and bustle of the port which was a sea of humanity at the crossroads of world trade.

The BI was not just another shipping company in Bombay and the Gulf; it was an institution. For example, many of the charts produced today by the Admiralty owe their origins to surveys and charts produced by the early BI captains in the mid 19th century. One did not serve on a BI ship but in one. The uniform buttons and cap badge depicted the reverse side of the Indian Mutiny Medal granted to BI by Queen Victoria. Curry would always be eaten with a spoon, something I still do to this day. In many of the ports that we visited BI had block membership of premier clubs that the officers could attend, such as the Boat Club in Karachi and the Gymkhana Club in Bahrain. Bombay was always a good run ashore with the Beach Kandi swimming pool where many expats would spend their afternoons, and of course there was the BI Club itself where officers passing through could stay in pleasant clean surroundings and have a game of billiards and a nice drink at the bar. The state of Gujarat was dry but many restaurants would serve alcohol if you were a licensed alcoholic. Such licences could be easily obtained from the Doctor at the BI Club for just a few rupees. In the Club the favourite tipple was gin and freshly squeezed limejuice. Such traditions die hard and recently, whilst entertaining on the Cable Ship Alert, I was asked for a gin and lime by a Captain from Trinity House. On asking which BI ships he had served in we were both delighted to discover that he had in fact relieved me aboard the *Bulimba* in Tilbury in 1969.

The Club also owned a very nice sailing boat available for the use of Officers. She was a 26-foot long half decked keelboat rather similar to the Solent Sunbeams still sailing today in clubs in the UK. She came with her own tindal (bosun's mate) who kept her in pristine condition and who, for a handful of rupees, would ensure that there was all the necessary food and drink for a delightful picnic. In later years whilst serving as second mate in the *Dumra* I made much use of this excellent facility that the Company provided free for our entertainment.

Leaving Bombay we called at Cochin and Madras before passing through the Straights of Singapore into the true Orient. Singapore was very different then to the city of high finance and high-rise skyscrapers it has become today. The Government was in the throes of breaking away from the newly formed Federation of Malaysia. I think that Raffles Hotel could have been one of the tallest buildings on the island. Little did we know then that this tiny island about the size of the Isle of Wight would become of such major importance by the turn of the century.

Hong Kong and Japan were pure magic to me. Japan had yet to shrug off the yoke of the Second World War and the yen was so weak that one could get one thousand to the pound, and even more through the moneychangers in Hong Kong. By drawing one hundred pounds from my wages at Hong Kong and seeking out the best rate of exchange I could make sufficient profit to pay for my run ashore in Hong Kong. But Japan, although very cheap in those days, showed all the signs of an industrious nation who would dominate world trade in a few years. I remember that air-conditioning in cars, which had not been dreamed of in the UK, was commonplace there. On my return home I mentioned to my father that I could see Japan leading the world in car manufacture and ship building in a few years' time. His reply was that I was talking rubbish and that these industries were the backbone of British trade and would always be thus.

After discharging our cargo of raw materials at Kobe, Osaka and Yokohama we loaded manufactured goods for India and the Gulf. This included a stop at Nagoya the home of Norataki China distinguished by the picture of the geisha secretly hidden in the bottom of the cup.

Japan had its fare share of industrial problems though. Trade and finance were so interwoven that we had to be back in Kobe, our main loading port, by the last day of the month ready to start loading on the first. This would establish the shippers right to sell his cargo once it was loaded aboard ship. Failure to meet this date would deny him this option for another month, thus incurring costly penalties. Once the cargo was loaded a 'mate's receipt' would be issued by the ship. This piece of paper would become a legal document and prove ownership of that cargo. The ownership could change several times during the voyage. The longshoreman unions dominated the waterfront in Japan and unless the correct wheels were lubricated ships could suffer crippling delays in waiting for a berth.

On leaving Japan we called at Shanghai in China. This was the time of the Red Revolution in China and it felt very uncomfortable being there with Chairman Mao's Red Guards prominent everywhere. As the pilot boarded the ship he was accompanied by a number of soldiers. Sailing up the river was quite hazardous, as we were not allowed to use any electronic devices such as Radar or depth sounders. At one stage a Guard appeared on the bridge threatening to shoot one of the Indian stewards. The interpreter called for the ship to be stopped immediately. This man was accused of operating secret surveillance equipment and the ship would be impounded. I was sent with the Chief Steward to investigate and discovered a cluster of excited soldiers looking into the glass of a front-loading washing machine. The situation was quickly rectified and we were allowed to proceed up river.

We had been lucky to clear the situation so easily however, others were not as fortunate. The next BI ship to call at Shanghai after us,

Mum, Nana, Anne and me

At the beach hut

Author aged 8

Catch of the day

First command

DECLARATION.

I DECLARE (i) that the person to whom this Discharge Book relates has satisfied me that he (she) is a seaman and (ii) that the photograph affixed bearing my official stamp is a true likeness of that person, that the signature within is his (her) true signature, that he (she) possesses the physical characteristics entered within and has stated to me the date and place of his (her) birth as entered within.

Signature of Supt. at Mercantile Marine Office—

- 1 OCT 1959

GLASGOW

Date 9/9/59

Photograph of Holder

R712696

M.M.O. Embossing Stamp

Christchurch Harbour

My Father and Sister Susan

suffered badly at the hands of the notorious Red Guard. The ship was accused of some petty offence by the authorities and the Captain was taken ashore and publicly humiliated and forced to make a public apology. The effect on the Captain was devastating and he was a broken man. BI immediately removed Shanghai from its itinerary.

One thing in particular that did impress me about Shanghai were the tents that they rigged over the hatches. Hatch tents are quite common in the Far East where heavy rainfall can catch out the unwary and ruin the cargo. These tents however did not just cover the cargo hold but with a ridge suspended between two derrick heads stretched right out over the quayside. Thus cargo work could continue even in the heaviest of downpours.

I did three trips on the *Chyebassa* before having to be rushed into hospital in Hong Kong. Having eaten ashore I picked up some strange virus and was taken off the ship just before sailing. The Peak Hospital was very comfortable and having a private room with a balcony I had magnificent views down into Aberdeen Bay and the floating restaurants. Having cleared up the problem relatively quickly the doctors would not allow me to leave Hong Kong as they expected a repeat of the symptoms. I was however allowed to leave hospital and move into an hotel in Kowloon. I had no sooner entered my hotel room than an Army Major contacted me. Unknown to me BI had advised my parents of my situation and Mother had contacted my Aunt and Uncle, who being Army personnel had contacted their friends in Hong Kong. The Major and his family were extremely kind and hospitable. I spent many evenings at their house and on one occasion was taken by an army patrol into one of the ancient cities in Kowloon that are never visited by tourists.

Word always spreads rapidly in the marine environment and I was also contacted by the Officers from the *Rajula*, one of the BI Eastern Service Passenger Ships that was refitting in Hong Kong at that time. I was immediately accepted by these guys who made sure that I was never lonely in a strange country. I remained in Hong Kong for four weeks and as had been expected the virus returned. Bent double with stomach cramps I crawled into the doctor's waiting room. This time they were able to identify the problem and within a few days I was as right as rain and out celebrating Chinese New Year with my friends. I was put on the next westbound ship and returned to Bombay where I joined the *Chakrata* on the Gulf–Australia run.

This ship had been through a bad time and had become a very unhappy ship. The Captain and several of the Deck Officers were changed but there remained a degree of interdepartmental mistrust and disharmony. Like the other C class ships the Officers' Lounge was at the after end of the boat deck but it was never used. Someone had started to build a bar but it was only half completed. The furniture was all set out around the edges of the room and the whole place was very inhospitable. With the Captain's permission I set too and tidied the place up. I had a couple of stewards to assist me and we soon cleaned the carpet and bulkheads and repositioning the furniture to make the room more inviting. Chippy helped me complete the bar and with a couple of ice-boxes filled with cold beers I announced that the new lounge bar was open for business. Just that little bit of basic housework had transformed a barrack like room into a comfortable pleasant rest area. Our new bar was an instant success and the atmosphere aboard the ship improved dramatically.

The lounge became the centre of social life and cabin drinking was eradicated. By the time we returned to Bombay from the Gulf our ship had become a very happy one. Once again I was introduced to the Superintendent, who allocated funds for a sink with hot and cold water to be fitted behind the bar, and I was given a wad of cash to refurbish the bar with glasses, pictures etc when we reached Australia.

Our first Australian port was Melbourne and we soon found a wholesaler where we were able to purchase glasses and other essentials for the bar. The young lady who sold them to us even offered to come down to the ship and help us break them in. I must say I was a little disappointed when she brought her husband along but I guess that served me right. As it turned out they were a lovely couple who gave us plenty of connections and we were promised a swell party on our return. Sydney was our next port and we had a swell time there. Word had already reached there by the time we arrived and we were soon besieged by offers of parties. It was amazing that what had been a miserable ship had changed so much and we were having a great time. There was still somewhat of a colonial style to Aussie life in those days and *'people from back home'*, as they called us were still very welcome.

It seemed as if life was one big holiday but we worked hard as well. Fortunately labour costs were very high then and overtime came at a huge cost and was to be avoided unless essential. This was great for us as it gave us freedom in the evenings and at weekends. In total we spent close on six weeks on the Aussie Coast.

Whilst we were in Bombay I learned that my cousin Roger had emigrated to Australia. Trying to find him would be almost impossible as the only forwarding address I had was his Bank in Melbourne. Not to be deterred I wrote, giving him our itinerary. By the time we reached Fremantle I had given up hope of meeting him. On our first evening I was walking along the deck checking that the hatches were secured after the dockers had left, when I saw two very unsavoury looking aborigines climb out of a decrepit old Ute (utilitarian vehicle) and approach the gangway with arms flailing and shouting some strange language. Anticipating trouble I headed for the gangway myself. I was aghast to discover that these two thoroughly disreputable looking characters were Roger and his mate. They had been shearing on a farm in the outback and had just finished their quota of two thousand sheep that morning, only to jump in the Ute and drive over three hundred miles on dirt roads to reach us. With no air-conditioning and temperatures in the high 30s and with the windows open it was not surprising that they were caked in red dirt. With a shower and change of clothes they looked almost human and the Captain allowed them to stay onboard for the duration of our stay in Fremantle. Life aboard ship can be quite insular and it was not surprising that these two reprobates became very popular with the rest of the Officers relating their tales of the outback and aborigines, most of which I am sure were mere figments of Roger's imagination.

The run back up to the southern tip of Ceylon was rather boring as ours was an unusual route, passing very few other ships. I always looked forward to sighting passing ships, especially at night when we would converse using the Aldis lamp. That flickering light starting with the call-signal AA AA AA and then the invitation – . . . – as 'what ship?', 'where bound?', would be the precursor to a welcome relief of the ocean navigator's boredom of routine watch keeping. I always looked forward to speaking to passing ships by Morse light. Not only did it help pass the time but gave useful practice for the Board of Trade examinations. Later MF and then VHF radio took the place of light signalling. I well remember crossing the Bay of Biscay on the *Malatian* where because she was under 1,600 tons we did not carry a radio officer and the bridge Watchkeeper kept the radio watch. We would always know that we were approaching Cape Finistere when the radio became saturated with Vigo, Vigo, Vigo, Vigo, Vigoooo, as the Spanish fishermen tried to connect with the coast radio station. When VHF radio came to the fore it unfortunately gave the idiot fraternity the opportunity to misuse the radio frequencies to transmit disgusting and totally inappropriate rubbish.

Looking back to my apprenticeship days I remember one occasion when the Aldis lamp was put to good use. Another Apprentice from our Company had fallen from a liberty boat and drowned in Hamburg harbour. Being the next ship to call at that port we were selected to carry the casket containing his body back to the UK. As we were a light ship and trimmed heavily by the stern it was quite an uphill climb as I walked up the fore' deck past No 1 hatch where the box lay. I was relieving the lookout on the foc'sle head and was not looking forward to my lonely two-hour vigil. This was the 12 till 4 watch, known by mariners as the graveyard watch. The minutes and hours seem to drag by very slowly and the mind plays tricks on one's sensibility.

The lookout would signal to the bridge by ringing the ship's bell when sighting a ship. I was standing there in quiet contemplation when the bell struck once: the signal for a light on the starboard bow. I looked around to see who was messing about but could find no one, but a light did soon appear to starboard. As we got further out to sea the ship began to rise and fall on the swell. Just as I was getting my nerve back the bell struck again, this time two strokes, and sure enough a light appeared to port. Again I searched the foc'sle; again to no avail, and I was starting to become rather nervous with that coffin only feet from where I was standing. When the bell struck again that was it. I was off to the bridge to report to the Second Mate. I was called some choice names by a very unsympathetic Mate who summoned the standby watch-keeper to accompany me back to my place of duty. I was telling the seaman the details of what had happened when, as we got level with No 1 hatch, the bell rang again by itself. The big burly seaman took off at speed with me following close behind. When we arrived back on the bridge the Second Mate was beside himself with mirth. Shining the Aldis Lamp on the foc'sle he illuminated the bell. As the bows rose on the swell due to our unusual trim the bell was swinging back on its gooseneck and striking the upright post. I felt very sheepish, as did our big burly seaman.

On approaching the Ceylon coast I witnessed a strange phenomenon of what appeared to be lights under the water. The light would first appear as a small intense glow which grew in brightness and spread out as it rose to the surface. I believe it was caused by phosphorescence given off by plankton which was brought to the surface by the mixing of two ocean currents. I had seen phosphorescent trails in the hot waters around Borneo where the water was disturbed by boats with outboard motors. Plankton plays a very important part in the food chain and is very temperature sensitive. As a boy I marvelled at the phenomenon created by these microscopic creatures in the water of Christchurch harbour. At a certain time of year (usually early summer) the water would become very brown then suddenly it would clear giving superb visibility so that one could not only see the seabed but all the fish swimming around. Just as quickly it would become cloudy again. Sometimes this would be accompanied by white frothy foam like soap suds. It was apparently due to the water temperature reaching a critical point and the plankton engaging in a frenetic breeding cycle.

Calling at Bombay and Karachi the *Chakrata* then headed into the Gulf where the temperature and humidity rose to summer levels. I had completed my two and a half years on Eastern Service and was very excited to receive a telegram from London to say that I was to be relieved at Kuwait to fly home for leave. This was a totally new experience for me and as the day drew nearer I could hardly contain myself. Leaving all my shipmates I was taken off to the airport and took what was to be the first of many flights. Today I dislike flying but that initial trip was so exciting. Two and a half years is a long time to be away from my family and friends. The first thing that struck me when arriving at London Heathrow was the dramatic change in fashion. Today Australia (which was where I had just come from) is abreast of world fashion but in those days it had still a colonial regard to such matters and change was slow. Mary Quant had stamped her ideas on London fashion and the mini skirt was evident everywhere. We were well into the swinging sixties and the UK was still hyper from their success in the world cup. Mum and Dad were waiting for me in arrivals and it was a very emotional reunion. I don't think I stopped talking the whole way home in the car, but one thing I do remember clearly was how very green the English countryside looked on that day in early May.

3

CHANGING TIMES

On my return to the UK I lost no time in acquiring myself a boat. My firefly dinghy had been sold during my absence and having accumulated six months leave I wanted a small cruiser to spread my wings. GRP or fibreglass as it was more commonly referred to in those days had not yet become established and most boats were still built of wood, especially plywood. I found a little 18-foot Silhouette class bilge-keeler fitted with a small Stuart Turner inboard engine that suited my aspirations. She had the name of *Fairy Queen*, taken from Shakespeare's *A Midsummer Night's Dream*. I wouldn't even have minded Titania but not Queen of the Fairies. I had to have a new name and when a friend suggested *Little X* then I jumped at the idea. For those who don't remember, Silhouette was a brand of ladies undergarments with Little X being their most popular girdle.

I bought her from a little yard in Poole and sailed her round to Christchurch on our maiden voyage. That little boat and I went all over the Solent exploring all the little creeks and harbours. It was a wonderful hot summer and I remember one particularly fine day sailing into the Newtown River. There were a couple of boats pulled up on the sand just outside the entrance and a small family group playing in the shallow water. I returned their waves as I nonchalantly sailed passed. I was admiring one of the boats that had an unusually long double chined planning hull. It was when I recognised Uffa Fox and knew that the boat that had so caught my interest was *Fairy Fox,* a most radical design of boat that he had built for Prince Philip, that I realised that the family party was none other than our Royal Family. It was so nice to see them behaving so naturally like any ordinary family with no intrusive paparazzi to impose on their serenity.

The Stuart Turner engine was typical of its type and at times was difficult to start. Once started it would run beautifully, but being a two stroke there was always the problem of separation between the petrol and oil, plus when hot it just refused to fire. I kept a ready supply of spare spark plugs, that helped, but it wasn't always convenient to change the plug at a time that required the use of engine power.

I had some good times and some scary ones in *Little X*. One Sunday morning I entered in a race from Mudeford to the Lymington Spit buoy and back. Peter an old friend who was a sports teacher at a local school was crewing for me and we were not taking the race very seriously, being possibly the slowest boat in the race. The visibility was poor with a light breeze from the east as we crossed the start line and tacked offshore. One by one all the other boats tacked back inshore leaving us on our own with a plan to pick up the last of the flood tide running up the Needles Channel. Just as we approached the Bridge Buoy off the Needles the wind started to increase and a lumpy sea got up. The wind continued to increase and veered to the South. The sea conditions rapidly deteriorated over the Shingles Bank and we opted to give up the race and run back into Christchurch. As we bore away the wind came round with us and I said 'I think we are going up the Solent whether we like it or not'. It was too rough to attempt to reef the mainsail and we just hung on hoping that nothing would break as we surfed up the Needles Channel. As we approached Hurst Castle the scene in front of us was of utter devastation. There were boats with sails blown out and others capsized, whilst one even sank. Barely able to control my own boat we were not in any position to help others and sailed through, leaving the Yarmouth lifeboat to pick up the unfortunate but lucky crews.

As we screamed up the Solent there was just one other boat left in the race and we approached the Spit Buoy about fifty yards behind her. At 24 feet in length she was rated much faster than us on handicap and I thought we had the race in the bag. The tide had by now turned but we were nicely closing on the buoy as the other boat rounded it. To our dismay the wind dropped as quickly as it had got up and with only ten yards from the buoy the tide started to pull us away from it. We were in a hopeless situation and we had no choice but to retire and return to Christchurch with the rest of the stragglers. Later, whilst quaffing a few pints at the bar, the other crews commented that when the storm hit them they were all worried for our safety, knowing that we had stood on out to the Needles. What a brave sight we had made coming out of the mist and surfing up the Channel through Hurst Narrows with the sails stretched to near breaking point. Little did they know just how scared we both had been out there in the rough water at the Bridge. A phone call to the Coastguards amazed us all when we learned that the lighthouse keeper on the Needles had recorded 45 knots of wind at the peak of the storm. I was very pleased with my little boat and the way that she had behaved. I would not like to repeat it though.

At the end of the summer I returned to my studies and by Christmas sat for my First Mate's Certificate, at which I was successful. With my leave coming to an end I was posted to the *Chantala* on the UK to East Africa service. I had become engaged before we left the UK with the intention of getting married in early summer. I did not enjoy the *Chantala,* which was a cadet training ship carrying 50 cadets. My cabin was directly above the cadet's dormitory and I frequently heard the sound of bullying emitting from there. I had fallen out with the Cadet Training Officer, who condoned the bullying, and I was told by the Captain not to interfere. When told that during my off-watch time I was responsible for teaching navigation whilst the CTO sunned himself on deck I had a sense of humour failure.

We entered some very interesting ports in East Africa like Dar es Salaam and Mombasa and the lovely spice island of Zanzibar. It was in Mombasa that I made what could have been a very embarrassing mistake. There were at least four other BI ships in port making a brave sight along the waterfront all with their black funnels with two white bands. It was a company tradition that when more than one of the company's ships were in port together, the senior ship would give the lead for raising and lowering flags. As we were senior ship and I was duty watch (most of the Officers were ashore at a football match) I prepared for flags. The senior ship would break out the numeral five at precisely five minutes before sunset with the other ships hoisting the Answering Pennant. Then at sunrise the flags would all be lowered together. Having calculated the time of sunset I called the Sukunni to the bridge. We raised the rolled up numeral five to the yardarm and at the calculated time pulled the halyard allowing the flag to fly out in the wind. Looking around I was surprised then concerned that none of the other ships had responded. Suddenly the sun broke through the clouds and it became very apparent that my calculations were wrong and that the sun was indeed not about to set. I was one hour too soon. Hurriedly we lowered the numeral five and bundled it up ready to repeat the operation in one hour's time. Fortunately no one had noticed and my mistake remained a secret between the Sukunni and me.

During my trip on the *Chantala* I received a letter from my father telling me that we were carrying a parcel of timber for his company. A customer had approached him asking for some timber that only originated in what was then Rhodesia. As there were supposedly strict trade sanctions imposed on all produce from Rhodesia at that time, he had been in the belief that this timber was unobtainable. Enquiries soon revealed that this wood under a different name and at a highly inflated price could be obtained via a neighbouring country and thus it ended up on our ship. It certainly makes one wonder who these sanctions helped and who suffered.

I clearly did not fit in to the regime of the cadet training ships and was not surprised to receive a telegram saying that I would be posted to another ship on my return to the UK. At least this gave me the opportunity to get married and have a honeymoon before joining my next ship, the *Chupra*. I was destined to sail on the same class of ship, all of which had names starting with the letter C. The day before we sailed from London my wife announced that she was pregnant, which news I passed on to Personnel who promised that they would try to keep me on a home line ship. I was therefore devastated on our arrival in Colombo three months later to be told that the *Chupra* was transferring to Eastern Service. The thought of another two and a half year tour was horrendous. This was no basis to start a married life with a baby expected shortly. Personnel stuck their heels in leaving me no option but to resign from the company. There followed a dreadful six months and I eventually arrived home to be greeted by my four week old daughter. That year had caused a terrible strain on both my wife and me that was ultimately to wreck the marriage.

From Colombo we had loaded in East Pakistan for Australian and New Zealand ports. I had thoroughly enjoyed my earlier trips to Oz but there was a heavy cloud hanging over me this time. We arrived in Auckland on a Sunday just before Christmas. In those days at weekends New Zealand just shut down, and as there was no cargo working and I knew nobody ashore I elected to be Duty Officer. The ship was like a ghost ship with everybody else ashore, when I was called to the telephone. The caller identified himself as being a former BI Second Officer now emigrated to New Zealand, who wondered if he knew anybody on board. Running through the list of Officers we drew a blank until he asked my name. He very excitedly reminded me that we had once met in Cochin when our respective ships had been in port together. We had gone ashore for a meal that I remembered was Chicken Piri Piri and we had eaten it with our fingers in true Indian style.

Tony and his wife Anne came down to the ship and later took me to their home where they entertained me most royally and tried their best to lift my spirits. They were a wonderful couple and I owed them a lot for their friendship.

From Auckland we were ordered to Quelimane in Mozambique, but before we could reach there the poor old *Chupra* suffered a serious engine breakdown passing through the Bass Straits and had to be towed into Melbourne. We were put onto Princes pier in the centre of town and remained there for 24 days. Apparently one unit of the engine was out of alignment and despite all manner of technical experts becoming involved the problem was unsolved until I casually made a remark to the Chief Engineer. I had been doing a routine survey of number 4 hold when I noticed a two-inch gap between the steel side to the propeller shaft tunnel and the deck plating. That had been on our arrival in Melbourne, but some ten days later the gap had mysteriously closed itself. I had been musing over this and had reached the conclusion that in the intervening ten days we had taken on fuel and fresh water. I suggested to the Chief Engineer (a very gruff Geordie) that at the time of the engine breakdown we were in the same condition as when the ship had been towed off the sandbank in East Pakistan. Could this be the cause of his problems? With his usual bonhomie he said 'what the hell did I know about engineering?' and returned to his cabin where he was in discussion with the Lloyds Surveyor. A few minutes later he came rushing back to say that I was F . . . ing right and to get the Captain back on board. I never did get any thanks or recognition for solving his problem.

With the engine repaired we set course once again for Mozambique. Whilst on passage I received a telegram saying that I was to be relieved in Quilermane and to fly to Calcutta to join the *Bombala* on route to London. Due to political difference at that time between Portuguese East Africa and India it was not possible to fly directly between those two countries and a more indirect route was selected for me. My itinerary took me to Salisbury (Rhodesia), Lisbon, Frankfurt, Beirut and Karachi before I finally arrived in Calcutta. As I had my full seagoing kit with me it was just short of a miracle that all my bags arrived with me at my destination. Whilst I was waiting for my flight at Frankfurt and hearing the boarding announcements for London bound flights I was highly tempted to skip it and go home where my wife was about to give birth. Realising that I owed it to my family to have a job to support them I stuck to my schedule. I know that today my decision would have most likely been very different.

When I did eventually arrive in Calcutta I was exhausted after four days of travel and was collected and taken to an hotel. It was there that I met a BI Captain who was also changing ship. He had heard that I had resigned and asked me why. Close to tears with tiredness and emotion I told him my story. It was a couple of years later that I discovered that this stranger had been so incensed by my story that he had cancelled his flight and gone instead to the BI offices in Calcutta, once the headquarters of the BI empire, and had relayed the events to the Senior Director. Four days later, having sailed from Calcutta I received a telegram from the Director of Personnel in London to say that he was personally in contact with my family and that my wife and baby daughter were both doing well and were looking forward to my return. I owed that Captain a great deal for his kindness and consideration in intervening on my behalf with the Personnel Department, and have tried to model myself on his example.

I was met at Tilbury by my father-in-law and taken home to a highly emotional reception.

I needed a further six months sea time to allow me to sit for my Master's Certificate and I had little option but to return cap in hand to BI, and with a written promise to get me home in six months in my hand I joined the *Dumra* on the colourful Bombay to Persian Gulf service.

The *Dumra*, despite being only 398 feet long and 4,500 tons deadweight, carried 1,537 passengers. Her voyage started at Bombay and she called at eight ports before arriving at Basra at the top of the Persian Gulf and then retracing her path. We carried a considerable cargo in addition to the passengers and their belongings. Walking around the tween decks was an experience. Families would mark out their territory by hanging blankets up to give them some meagre seclusion, but there was little privacy on those crowded decks. Her passenger licence required so many square feet (I believe it was eighteen) of deck space per passenger but this did not include the hatches. Once the cargo work was completed and the hatches boards were replaced there was a stampede to secure additional space. There were frequent scuffles and tensions would run high between the different races and creeds.

In addition to the usual migratory Arab and Indian workforce travelling up and down the Gulf we occasionally had what we referred to as Unwashed Europeans. These early backpackers, in search of drugs, were just about the dregs of humanity. Most of them had sold all their possessions including their passports in the search for anything to feed their habits. They were despised by everyone and not surprisingly BI would not allow women in this group, although some did get through the security.

Despite the high numbers and the stifling heat of the Gulf these were very happy and popular little ships. At the end of each bridge watch (mine was the 4–8) I would take a walk around the decks before going to my cabin. I would usually be joined on my perambulation by the Security Officer, whose job it was to maintain law and order. Jim was an ex Palestine Police Officer from the days of the postwar conflict in Israel and he would take no messing.

Security Officers had been introduced to these ships when the *Dumra*'s sister-ship the *Darra* had been bombed by Yemeni rebels off of Dubai. The ship had been embarking passengers in the anchorage when an unexpected gale which had caused other ships to drag anchor forced the *Darra* to weigh anchor and steam offshore. There were hundreds of additional people on board, as the departing passengers had yet to be landed, and in addition there were the stevedores who had been handling the cargo. Some time before midnight a bomb, planted in the tween decks adjacent to the engine room, had exploded, causing instant fire. The fire was fuelled by all the blankets and bedding hung up in the tween decks and with a gale of wind fanning the flames fire quickly engulfed the ship. Even as the crew struggled to launch the lifeboats the tar in the deck seams was catching fire around their feet. At one stage the Second Officer and some crew lowered a lifeboat from the fore deck and took it to the stern where they climbed up ropes to get back on board to encourage passengers to jump in to the water where the waiting lifeboats would save them. There were many acts of gallantry made by very brave people that night. The death toll that stormy night reached 174 passengers, 14 Dubai shore staff and 24 crew but it was a miracle that many more people were not lost. Three Royal Navy frigates came to their assistance and sprayed the ship with hoses but the fire had too strong a hold and the ship finally sank under tow just to the north east of the anchorage. Every trip we would see her masts sticking up out of the water as we sailed past. A grim reminder of just how vulnerable those ships were.

I was always happy to get back to Bombay after our round trip of 24 days. I was there on one turn around during the festival of Diwali.

Diwali is a five-day Hindu festival which occurs on the fifteenth day of Kartika. Diwali means 'rows of lighted lamps' and the celebration is often referred to as the Festival of Lights. During this time, homes are thoroughly cleaned and windows are opened to welcome Laksmi goddess of wealth. Candles and lamps are lit as a greeting to Laksmi. Gifts are exchanged and festive meals are prepared. The celebration means as much to Hindus as Christmas does to Christians. Because there are many regions in India, there are many manifestations of the Diwali festival. In at least one area, the festival begins with Dhanteras, a day set aside to worship Laksmi. In the Indian culture, wealth is not viewed as a corruptive power. Instead, a wealthy person is considered to have been rewarded for good deeds of a past life. On the second day Kali, the goddess of Strength, is worshipped. This day also focuses on abolishing laziness and evil. On the third day (the last day of the year in the lunar calendar), lamps are lit and shine brightly in every home. The lamp symbolizes knowledge and encourages reflection upon the purpose of each day in the festival. The goal is to remember the purpose throughout the year. The fourth day of Diwali falls on the first day of the lunar New

Year. At this time, old business accounts are settled and new books are opened. The books are worshipped in a special ceremony and participants are encouraged to remove anger, hate, and jealousy from their lives. On the final day (Balipratipada) of the festival, Bali, an ancient Indian king, is recalled. Bali destroyed the centuries-old philosophies of Indian society. However, in addition to this, he is remembered for being a generous person. Thus, the focus of this day is to see the good in others, including enemies.

This is a lovely time to be in India as it captures so much of the Indian culture and I felt very honoured to witness it.

It was with a degree of sorrow that at the end of my six months I left the *Dumra*. I had a young family to be getting home to and study time for my master's certificate to look forward to. I thought that I would never return to India, but how wrong I was. I think that once you have experienced the magic of India a little part of it remains with you.

4

UNION CASTLE TO CABLE SHIPS

Clutching my brand new master's ticket in my hand I looked for a new job. Determined that I was not embarking on any more lengthy voyages that would take me away from my young family I got a job with Union Castle in Southampton. The passenger trade to South Africa was sorely depleted since its heyday when the lavender coloured hulls would occupy the majority of berths in the old docks in Southampton.

The fast mail run to the Cape still employed seven ships from their base at 102–104 berths in the new docks. A mail boat would sail at 1 p.m. every Friday with the incoming ship arriving at 7 a.m. on a Monday. We had a team of officers who would board the incoming vessel and relieve the sailing crew who would go immediately on leave, returning ten days later just before sailing day with the ship loaded and stored ready for the embarkation of passengers. We would be responsible for security of the vessel and watch over the discharge and loading of cargo and any repairs being undertaken. The ships always sailed exactly on time and it was a tribute to the organisation that annual refits and dry-dockings could be accommodated without delaying departure.

I had sold my boat to put the deposit down on a house in New Milton on the edge of the New Forest. The house was in easy walking distance of the station and I would daily make that picturesque run through the New Forest to Southampton. I would be reminded of my school days when majestic steam engines would haul our school train from Christchurch to Brockenhurst in the centre of the Forest, where we would walk up the leafy lanes to the Grammar School. Some of the old lines had been removed by the Beeching axe which closed many of the branch lines throughout Britain.

The next stop up from Christchurch was at the little village of Hinton Admiral, seat of the Merrick family who owned much of the real estate in Bournemouth. Local rumour has it that Sir George Merrick and his family (descendants of Sir Francis Drake) had the historic right to stop any train at the station of Hinton Admiral to board or leave it. This did not go down well with the new bureaucratic regime of British Rail Management in the Beeching era.

They wrote to Sir George saying that, with a need to increase efficiency, they would be closing the station and abrogate his right to stop trains for his own use. Sir George duly wrote back saying that he fully appreciated and applauded their attempts to improve the efficiency of the railways and that if they felt it uneconomic to retain the station, despite the area growing as a commuter belt, then close the station by all means and he would be grateful if they would remove their track from his land as soon as possible. This was of course the main line from Bournemouth to London and they had failed to appreciate the business acumen of Sir George's forefathers in retaining ownership of the land. Needless to say the station remains open to this day and I believe that the occasional express makes an unscheduled stop at Hinton Admiral.

During the winter months the mail ships would fetch in many thousands of tons of fresh fruit from The Cape. There were apples and pairs, oranges and lemons, peaches and apricots and various varieties of melons. Any broken cases would be swept up and binned as rubbish. On most days I would return home with a grip full of exotic fruit for my family. My two daughters always had a ready supply of such wonderful fruit.

Some of the ships were fitted with bulk liquid tanks in which they carried wine in the form of sherry. The Shore Bosun was responsible for stripping down the lines on completion of discharge. There was always a glass of wine left over at the end of the exercise. The Wine shippers said that their product was never diluted but I have never tasted anything like that sherry elsewhere. It was magnificent.

The Dock Strike of 1973 threatened to disrupt the sailing schedules but the Management circumvented the problems by using shore staff and management to offload passenger baggage from the incoming ship and then sending her to Antwerp for discharge of her cargo. The ship affected was the SA *Vaal* previously named *Transvaal Castle.* At 37,697 tons she was a big ship and sailing on her to the Continent as Second Officer was quite an experience. I remember coming on watch at midnight to find the ship racing through the Dover Straits at 22 knots. This was indeed scary stuff. Despite all the disruption we still managed to sail her on schedule the following week.

During my career at sea I have seen many different cargoes shipped from and to a variety of places. From the general cargoes that we carried outward from the UK to the Mediterranean to thousands of miles of submarine telecommunications cables, they all had their own peculiarities. I think however that the most difficult and demanding cargos were passengers; they could be pleasant one moment and a total pain in the butt the next. They were never satisfied with where their baggage was stowed and certainly liked to complain about their accommodation whenever given a chance.

Sailing out from Bombay on the little *Dumra* was an experience in its own right. Indian law required people of Indian nationality, when travelling as a cabin passenger, to pay a tax on any possessions taken out of the country, but if travelling unberthed as a deck passenger they were exempt. These deck passengers would file up the gangway carrying their bedding roles and bundles of possessions. For many these bundles were the sum of their worldly possessions.

Many travellers would come aboard as deck passengers and the moment that the ship sailed ask to be upgraded to cabin class. This was very popular with the Purser and Butler who would capitalise on this very lucrative trade. Of course the Purser accept most graciously the difference in cost whilst the Butler would charge the passengers for supplying Indian food direct to their cabins.

The ship was equipped with several galleys. The saloon galley supplied European food to the Dining Saloon for the cabin passengers and Ship's Officers. In the tween decks that ran right through the ship from bow to stern and where most of the deck passengers lived were galleys catering for the different cultural needs of Hindu, Moslem, Christian and Vegetarian tastes. This food was delicious and frequently I would ask for a plate or two of mouth-watering curry.

The Papayanni ships were all designed for the citrus fruit trade with large powerful ventilators on deck to suck up the citrus gases given off by the cargo. They would also carry potatoes from the Med to the UK when the markets required. Most years imported potatoes would carry a tariff during the UK season to protect the home market.

I remember one year when for some reason the UK crop had failed waiting at Famagusta in Cyprus for the tariff to be fixed, this was usually around the 16 June. That year every available ship was rushed to Cyprus to capitalise on the market. The price of potatoes in the UK had gone through the roof and there was good money to be made. I also carried potatoes from Egypt and of all places Ibetha. That of course was long before the Hippy invasion of the island and the spelling was changed to the more exotic Ibiza.

We once carried a large consignment of baled waste paper to Corfu. Again this was long before the holiday trade took over the island. The paper went into the production of brown cardboard cartons for shipping black fruit (currants, sultanas and raisins) that were shipped to UK and Near Continental countries in huge amounts.

In the days of the Union Castle ships the two fast cargo passenger ships *Southampton Castle* and *Good Hope Castle* would frequently carry livestock out to South Africa. I always liked being involved with the loading of thoroughbred racehorses that when seen at the racecourse are all jumpy and skittish but when not given their oats and high protein feed would be so beautifully behaved. We had special heavy wooden stalls that they would be loaded into and I would often go into the stall with a horse whilst it was being loaded. I wasn't so keen going in with the stud bulls but even they were much less aggressive than their reputation makes out.

There would be some interesting homeward cargoes too. One was a steam engine from one of the South African railways being brought back to the UK for restoration. I recall watching a beautiful Rolls Royce loaded aboard the *Good Hope Castle* on the fated voyage when the ship caught fire and was almost lost. When she was towed back to Europe and the hatches were opened up, the car was just a small pile of melted metal.

She was on her outward voyage bound for Cape Town, calling at Ascension and Saint Helena. She had left Ascension shortly before her sister ship arrived at St Helena north bound and they expected to pass each other the following day. St Helena reported that they had not heard from the *Good Hope Castle*, and nothing was seen of her by the *Southampton Castle* by the time she arrived at Ascension. The ship had just disappeared. In actual fact she had caught fire and had been unable to send out a radio distress message as the bridge and Radio Room had immediately filled with noxious gases given off by burning Formica.

The fire had started at the top of the Engine Room during the night. Although the initial fire was quickly contained it was not realised that the heat had ignited the compound on the deck above the space and this had slowly simmered until suddenly erupting into a second fire. The ship's total supply of CABA bottles was soon used up and the crew could not get into the accommodation to fight the fire that was quickly spreading. The Captain had ordered the entire crew and passengers into the lifeboats and abandoned ship. Being thousands of miles from land they remained close to the ship, anticipating the early arrival of their sister-ship. The crippled ship, although stopped in the water, was carried off her track by strong ocean currents, which was why the other vessel had failed to see her. This was an area of the South Atlantic well away from usual shipping routes and seldom frequented by shipping. It was fortunate that a passing tanker, on an unusual route, saw the smoke and went to investigate. Once the plight of the *Good Hope Castle* was known, a Clan Line ship was diverted to collect the crew and take them to Cape Town, whilst a tug was despatched to extinguish the fire and tow the gutted ship back to Bilbao in Spain. Surprisingly the Engine Room, which was where the fire had started, was relatively unscathed and the superstructure was rebuilt and the ship returned to service.

When I was on the *Chakrata* in BI on one trip from Sydney we went up to Newcastle to load railway tyres. These were steel rims for the wheels of rolling stock on the Iraq Railways. They were particularly difficult to stow. They obviously had to be laid flat but they were so shiny and slippery that when the ship rolled they would slide from side to side if not properly secured. Should one have broken loose it could possibly have gone clear through the hull plating.

That same voyage at Adelaide we loaded Holden cars that had to be unloaded and then reloaded at Fremantle, where the holds were filled with bagged wheat. One Chief Officer had decided that to save space and avoid difficult lashing of the cars sitting on the bagged wheat he would fill in the spaces between the cars with more bags to stop them from moving.

Now cars have sprung suspension and when the ship moved the cars moved. When we came to discharge the cars in the Gulf they were incredibly shiny. Every vestige of paint had been rubbed off the bodies by the movement between grain sacks and the cars.

After our redirection of the *Chupra* onto Eastern Service we went to Khulna and Chittagong, in what was then East Pakistan and now called Bangladesh, to load jute to be taken to Australia and New Zealand to be turned into sacks for the wool trade. There was civil war taking place in that country at that time and amongst the usual detritus floating in the harbour at Chittagong were a number of dead bodies, of which the authorities took little or no interest. Life there was very cheap.

Khulna is several miles inland from the coast on one of the many arms that form the delta of the Ganges, that amazing river that rising in the foot hills of the Himalayan carries the water of life to most of India.

On her previous voyage the *Chupra* had grounded on a sandbar in this river and had to be lightened by pumping out all her water ballast and fuel oil before she could be towed free. On this voyage we were more fortunate, but whilst loading our cargo most of the Officers suffered from a severe skin rash brought on by expose to pollen from the Jute Moth. The clouds of moth were drawn into the ship's air-conditioning system that only supplied warm air but was distributed about the accommodation through the Punka Louver System. The rash caused severe irritation and it wasn't until the ship reached Penang that, with copious supplies of ointment, were we able to eradicate the problem.

In BI we frequently carried onions. As they gave off a gas, which could be fatal if inhaled, and as we had no gas metres in those days, we were required to carry chickens to test the air in spaces where onions were stowed. One bird would be lowered into the space and if it was unaffected then it was deemed to be safe to enter the hold. The hens were well looked after by the deck crew and fattened up until the cargo was discharged when they would then go into the pot. It was traditional for the Sarang (Indian Bosun) to make curry with some of the chickens for the Officers' Dining Saloon. This was always a treat and far removed from anything bought today from an Indian Restaurant in the UK.

I had only joined the Union Castle team as a stopgap but remained there for four years until joining the Post Office Marine Division. Married life had made me give up my boating in favour of family activities. I exchanged my yellow wellies for gumboots. Not only did we have rabbits and chickens but horses, ponies and for a very short time a donkey. It is a strange fact of life that different people have totally different priorities.

One day whilst working in the Office of BT Marine in Southampton one of our ships was having problems in the Bay of Biscay. The CS *Alert* had been trialing a new hydraulic active grapnel in deep water. This huge grapnel weighing over a ton was designed to hook the cable on the seabed and cut the cable, holding onto one side, whilst releasing the other side. The cable could then be recovered to the surface.

Their activities, which included transmissions from the grapnel to the mother ship, had attracted the interest of a Russian Fishing Vessel. They had at times come extremely close to the *Alert* (less than one cable) and the Captain was getting concerned. We had contacted the Navy and Foreign Office and it transpired that the Navy were holding exercises nearby and they despatched a frigate to assist the *Alert*. An Officer from the frigate was transferred by helicopter to the *Alert*. The Captain was using scrambler telephone communications and sending coded signals.

All this must have only increased the Russians' determination to discover what was going on. They possibly thought that there was a submarine in distress on the bottom. Their interest was further aroused when after the frigate left the Aircraft Carrier *Ark Royal* came up over the horizon.

I was the Senior Seagoing Officer in the office the next day and had been handling simultaneously telephone calls from the Admiralty in London, Flag Officer Plymouth and The Foreign Office when my Clerical Officer came in to say that my wife needed to speak to me very urgently. Thinking that something serious had happened to one of my daughters I put everybody else on hold and picked up the call from my distressed wife who said, '*Where have you put the lice powder? Some of the chickens have lice and I can't find the powder anywhere.*' This matter obviously had to take precedence over the possible full scale international incident being enacted in the Bay of Biscay!!!

When people first learn that I had worked on cable ships they invariably ask if we use divers to repair the cables. The answer is of course no but we did use a number of submersibles.

Shortly before I first joined the Post Office Cable Ships there had been a dramatic rescue from a small manned submarine in waters South of Ireland. *Pisces 2* had been jetting in a transatlantic cable when a problem had sent the sub to the bottom unable to surface by herself. Various vessels were involved in the epic struggle to recover the sub with two people onboard. This included the Canadian Cable Ship *Sir John Biscoe.* The sub was eventually recovered after several days with the crew desperately short of air.

The drama was so interesting that it attracted the interest of the BBC who in 1999 made a documentary about it, with much of the filming being done aboard CS *Monarch* off Portland UK. I was in command of *Monarch* at the time and was very surprised to be told that I was required to play the part of Captain of the Mother ship. In fact a number of *Monarch*'s crew had their first taste of television acting that day. Of course none of us were paid for our appearances but it was a novel experience none the less.

As I watched the half hour long programme on the television I had to reflect back to that Navy Doctor's comments some forty years before. I had combated my stutter and was not only a Ship's Captain but had appeared on television as such.

5

CABLES UNDER THE SEA

My earliest recognition of cable ships was from my Observers Book of Ships. There were pictures of ships with strange shaped bows but my main recollection was that telegraph ships, as they were know in those days, had white hulls with a dark coloured band around them which signified their unusual deployment and the fact that they were tethered to the seabed by a thin strand of cable and were hampered in their ability to manoeuvre.

Being in the timber trade Dad had connections with Southampton Docks which in those days were run by British Rail, and he would bring home for me their monthly journal of shipping. I was fascinated by pictures and reports of all the ships visiting the port of Southampton, plying their trade to far off corners of the world. Sometimes I was lucky enough to be taken to Southampton by train where the track runs close to the KG5 dry dock. Sometimes if we were really lucky one of the Cunard Queens would be in dock. Their bows soaring high above the train track, the *Queen Elizabeth* and *Queen Mary* were the largest ships to use the port and were an awesome sight for any schoolboy. But I particularly recollect seeing the big white-hulled cable ships lying at the loading berth for the Standard Telephone Cables cable factory positioned close to the dry dock. They were like no other ship, without hatches for loading cargo, nor huge blocks of accommodation for passengers. They were certainly glamorous vessels and their white hulls made them look like big yachts.

The Fifties and Sixties saw a huge growth in the need for communications cables under the sea. The invention of the repeater that amplified the speech circuits down a telephone system made it possible to transmit speech for hundreds and then thousands of miles. The British Post Office had built a huge cable ship to meet the demands for international cable around the world. His Majesty's Telegraph Ship *Monarch*, as she was named, was a frequent visitor to Southampton, where she would load many thousands of miles of cable into her cavernous holds to take off to remote areas to lay down on the seabed. This ship was responsible for the laying of the Compac cable that linked the Commonwealth countries around the world. Sighting her from the train as she loaded her cable in Southampton had always intrigued me and I wondered at the technology that allowed people to speak to each other from thousands of miles apart.

Governmental reorganisation in the early Seventies gave the rights for worldwide cable laying to Cable & Wireless, then a government owned company, and restricted the Marine Division of the British Post Office to UK and Continental systems and cables terminating in the UK. The *Monarch* was sold to C&W and the Post Office was left with just three ships. *Monarch* was to finish her life as a station ship in Bermuda helping to maintain the transatlantic cable systems, a far cry from her historical eminence in spanning the world with cable linking up the Commonwealth.

It was from the bridge of the Union Castle flagship *Windsor Castle* lying at berth 102 that I first saw the CS *Alert* as she came into Southampton to load cable from the STC factory. I, like many others, thought that the days of submarine telecommunications cables were coming to a close as satellites took over their work. This was so very far from reality. Submarine cables were in their ascendance once more as they proved themselves to be more robust and giving better transmission. Should any part of a satellite become faulty it cannot be fixed in the way that cables can be. When one is talking on a satellite link there is a noticeable delay caused by the huge distances that the signal has to travel into space and back. Cables were to be given another huge boost by the introduction of Optical Fibre, which gave enormous increases in capacity. With the introduction of the Internet, the demand for capacity was to increase beyond all expectations.

Unfortunately, due to high risks of non-recognition in the fogs of the North Sea and Dover Straits, the Post Office ships had been painted orange with grey superstructure, which seriously detracted from their appearance. However *Alert* still looked an interesting vessel as she entered the Port. The days of the Union Castle passenger ships was coming to a close and I was looking for a new post. The allure of the cable ships interested me, particularly as the Post Office had just commissioned a new depot in Southampton, and a quick phone call secured me an interview that very afternoon. Within a couple of hours I was travelling home to inform my family that I had a new job.

Three days later I walked up the gangway of the *Alert* as a Navigating Officer. Still very much living under the shadow of the Civil Service, the Post Office Ships had a different rank structure to the Merchant Navy in general. The Bridge Officers were Navigators with a minimum of a 1st Mate's ticket, but usually a Master's certificate. After specialising in the art and mysteries of cable working they would ascend to Cable Officer and then Chief Cable Officer through to Captain. There was no Bosun but a Cable Foreman was the senior Petty Officer.

There was a tremendous amount to take in as we were loading cable for a new system running from Rome to Israel, passing through the Messina Straits. The system consisted of five loads, two of which were laid by CS *Alert* the other three by STC's own elderly *John W Macai*. The cable size varied from lightweight for the deep water, rising in size and weight to single, double and triple armouring for the shallow water where the cable was at its greatest risk. The system contained repeaters (torpedo-like casings housing amplifiers and weighing about a ton) that were carefully loaded and stacked in the Centre Castle ready to be jointed into the system. With one repeater every six miles there were about one hundred repeaters in each load. As each repeater was jointed into the system it had to be powered up and all the components checked.

The cable sections were coiled by hand into the ship's cable tanks each of which ran the full width of the vessel. The ends were bighted up into the Centre Castle ready for jointing to the cable. To the uninitiated like me it looked like a huge cat's cradle and I wondered how often a cross in the ends resulted in a huge knotted tangle. Fortunately and reflecting the expertise of the crew I have never seen this happen, but I believe it has happened on other ships. I believe at that time the cost of a repeater plus its cable section was about half a million pounds, and thus the entire system ran into many millions of pounds.

With our valuable cargo safely stowed we sailed from Southampton for Messina in Sicily. This was the second segment, the first having already been laid by the *John W Macai* with a weighted ground rope at the seaward end. Before starting to lay the Captain wanted to make a dummy run through the Messina Straits to check the Navigational system. The seabed in the Straits is very mountainous with peaks, valleys and gullies throughout its length. The route had been carefully surveyed using sophisticated depth sounding equipment and a Trisponder navigational system with stations set up along the shore. The Senior Officers were not happy with the system and spent several hours locked in debate with the Representatives from STC. In the end the decision was made to go ahead with the lay, but with the Cable Officers driving the ship whilst plotting our position by Trisponder we navigators plotted our position by conventional visual and radar positioning.

We passed out through the Northern end of the Straits into the Tyrrhenian Sea and sighted the volcanic island of Stromboli rising over three thousand feet above sea level. The onboard cable end had been passed out through the stern sheaves and along the ship's side to be pulled back in through the bow sheaves ready for jointing to the sea end of the already laid cable. We grappled for the ground rope and recovered the cable end over the bows, and after rigorous testing set about jointing the cable end to our load. It is vitally important that the ship holds station whilst this is going on as the cable can easily throw a loop which, when pulled tight, damages the cable.

The Cable Ship Alert had been specifically chosen for this lay as she had recently been fitted with a brand new concept of hydraulic cable engine. This consisted of sixteen pairs of wheels each about the size of a scooter wheel. The pressure between the sets of wheels was regulated by a combination of pneumatics and hydraulics. As a gas can contract under pressure whilst a liquid will not, by placing a small neoprene sack filled with gas into the hydraulic chamber, the wheels can be made to open automatically as external pressure is applied. The pressure between the wheels is adjusted by the hydraulics. When the wheels meet the resistance of an increased diameter in the cable, pneumatic sensors tell the wheels to open to adjust to the new diameter. Thus as a repeater, which is many times larger in girth than the cable, enters the wheels of the laying engine, the wheels automatically open to allow the repeater housing to pass through, whilst still maintaining the same grip on both cable and repeater. This cable engine having been designed by Post Office staff had totally revolutionised cable-laying.

After about eighteen hours with the cable powered up and the transmission staff monitoring the system through our load and back to the cable terminal in Rome we transferred the bight of cable from the bows to the stern and commenced laying. Again the angle of repose of the cable as it passes out over the stern is critical. Too much tension would leave the cable suspended on the seabed whilst insufficient tension would throw loops. As we were in deep water of over one thousand fathoms we started off laying lightweight cable, but as we approached the Straits of Messina the cable changed to single and then double armouring. It was critical that the correct amount of slack was laid out to position the triple armoured cable in the right place in the Straits. At one point a member of the STC team believing that we were laying too tightly came to the bridge and requested more slack. Half an hour later he returned in turmoil saying that his calculations were wrong and that we must now tighten up the system. The Captain, far from pleased but showing amazing calm, requested the engineers to increase the cable tension in the laying machinery. Suddenly there was a shout from the Chief Cable Officer that the cable had come out of the wheels of the cable engine. We had a runaway situation with the heavy double armoured cable pouring out over the stern. With men in the tank it was an incredibly dangerous situation. The Cable Engine Driver, a lovely totally unflappable Hebridean Scot, opened up all the pairs of wheels, and allowing the cable to drop back into position, started closing the wheels to bring the cable back under control. The ship had already been brought to a stop but a huge amount of cable had run away and needed to be recovered. We cut the cable, and transferring it to the bows, commenced recovering it. The expensive double armoured cable was not a pretty sight as it came in over the bow sheaves with kink after kink in the now useless cable. Once we had recovered the repeater from the section where the initial slack mistake had been made, we cut and buoyed off the cable whilst the damaged cable was cut out and replaced by spare sections.

Whilst the jointing and testing continued the ship steamed slowly around the Lipari Islands. During the long night hours of my watch I started to muse about stories of Stromboli and the Greek hero Odysseus, recalling my school days and the story of Scylla and Charybdis from Greek mythology. Scylla, that supernatural creature with twelve feet and six heads on long, snaky necks, each head having a triple row of shark like teeth, whilst her loins were girt with the heads of baying dogs, was purported to have her lair in a cave at the entrance to the Straits. Was she now lurking waiting for us? Had it been Charybdis who wrenched the cable from our grasp? It is amazing what the mind conjures up during those long hours of the graveyard watch.

Two days later we recovered our cable buoy and once more jointed our load onto the sea end in preparation to laying our cable through the Straits. Once again we slipped the bight of cable around the ship from the bow to the stern sheave and commenced paying out cable. As we entered the Messina Straits I saw the huge whirlpools and again was reminded of Charybdis.

As we made our way through the Straits it soon became apparent that something was amiss as the Trisponder positioning was different to our manual observations. We continued with the prepared survey route and eventually everyone breathed a sigh of relief when we were eventually clear and into open waters.

Once we had completed our section we slipped the cable end on a ground rope ready for the *Makai* to continue and we returned to Messina. Once berthed we checked our position against the Satellite Navigation System. This was the early version of the Transit System that was the forerunner of GPS. It took a room the size of a cabin to house all the computers, a far cry from the little hand-held systems in use today. To everyone's amazement we discovered that the satellites put our position several hundred metres east of the charted one. It later transpired that having positioned the Trisponder beacons on the Italian side of the Straits for the survey the planners had moved them to the Sicilian side for the lay to give a better cross. The satellite however showed an error in the charted position of Sicily. Unfortunately instead of laying the cable down the smooth surveyed route we had laid it over the peaks and troughs. Fortunately the ship was not at fault but it certainly took the gloss off of what should have been a super job well done. Maybe Charybdis had her way in the end!

We reached home before Christmas and in the New Year took on our second load. This lay was far more straightforward than the first, however we did raise some interest. We were approaching the position of the cable end south of Crete when we encountered the American Mediterranean fleet on exercises. We were called up by the lead destroyer who asked the usual: what ship, where bound – but when we replied – last port Malta, next port Malta – they became interested in us and asked us to go to VHF radio. Having explained our mission they bade us farewell, but when I asked them to relay to the vessel directly in front of us our intentions and that we were about to turn to commence grappling and would not hamper their course; they replied with, 'Tell him yourself, he's Russian'. It greatly amused us that with all their sophistication they had a Russian ship tagging along for the ride.

The *Alert* was for many years the flagship of the BT fleet. Primarily designed as a repair ship for the North Atlantic she was based at Southampton but was often called upon to cover other stations as well as laying cable. It was whilst serving as Chief Cable Officer on *Alert* that I sailed on my first tall ship. We were covering the Vigo station when the American Topsail Schooner *Pride of Baltimore* entered the bay. She made a very grand sight as she tacked back and forth across the bay. When she berthed very close to us it gave me an opportunity to meet the captain and crew. She had been built as a copy of the Chesapeake Bay Topsail Schooners who were famous as blockade-runners during the American War of Independence.

We were going out to undertake some trials of new equipment and returned just in time to see the schooner leave. As we were now berthed in a different part of the port Ricky our agent offered to take me around to see her depart. I was particularly interested in watching her manoeuvre with only very limited auxiliary power. Standing on the quayside as the crew prepared to depart I cast an appreciative eye over this lovely ship. The skipper seeing me standing there called up and invited my to go along with them. Their next port was Bayona, only a short distance away by car. Ricky said that his cousin, who was president of the Bayona Yacht Club, was on board and he would be prepared to bring me back that evening. With promises that Ricky would explain my absence to my Captain, the offer of sailing aboard such a lovely craft was just too much and I climbed down onto the schooner's deck.

It was a beautiful day with warm sunshine and a gentle breeze. Sailing backwards and forwards across the bay, watching the crew handle the sheets and braces was pure magic to me. She was superbly built of the finest materials. Her keel was made of Lignum Vitae and the taff-rail that went right around the bulwarks was of rosewood. I was intrigued to see that the small canons ranged along the side carried the insignia of the British Monarchy. They had been cast from moulds made from captured guns from the early eighteenth century. As we entered Bayona the captain fired off blank charges from a couple of the canon. It was not until on my way back to Vigo that I remembered that I had absconded from my duties. Fortunately Ricky had done an excellent job and Captain Roy said how envious he was of my day sailing aboard such a magnificent ship. Apparently they had all been watching us sailing across the bay and would to the man have given a lot to be in my shoes.

Whilst the *Alert* looked after the transatlantic cables, the UK home waters and North Sea were left to the CS *Iris* and CS *Monarch*, much smaller and very manoeuvrable little ships. It was whilst on the *Monarch* as Cable Officer (equivalent to second mate), that I had a most embarrassing experience in Holyhead harbour. One of the cables crossing to Ireland was faulty in the shallow waters of the harbour. Mike the Chief Cable Officer was conducting the repair from our workboat with the launch in attendance. We received a signal that some urgent stores were waiting for us in the Post Office and I set off in one of the lifeboats to collect them. I gave the boat's crew specific instructions to stand off whilst I went to collect the parcels. As it was a Sunday I felt secure that here in darkest Wales they could not get their hands on any alcohol.

Now Holyhead has an enormous tidal range and by the time I returned the ebb tide had just started. I called the boat in to a little stone jetty with a channel marked with withies. Their angle of approach alarmed me and before reaching the jetty the boat grounded. Wading out to the boat I soon realised that the two lads whom I had left in the boat were well inebriated. Clambering over the side of the boat I remonstrated with them and told them to grab boathooks and push the boat back into the channel. Within minutes it became obvious from the way the boat rocked back and forth on its keel that we were now high and dry. Calling the ship on my radio I asked the Duty Officer for the time of low water.

The answer was in three hours' time. Trying to conceal my chagrin I asked the Duty Officer to give my compliments to the Captain and advise him that we would not be back for another six hours. I could almost hear the cheer go up in the Officers' bar, as the cost of putting a boat aground was double drinks all round. By the time we made it back the work party had completed their cable operation and I was met by a very jovial Chief Officer who, with a broad grin handed me a chitty for a large number of beers.

Mike had been reminded of a time when we had been repairing a cable off the coast of Northern Ireland. We were on the *Monarch*'s predecessor the earlier *Iris*. Built during the war she was a funny little ship with twin screws but no thrusters. With low freeboard many was the time when we finished a repair with waves breaking over the bow whiskers and water running down the foredeck. We had a Captain who was of Polish extraction who found it very difficult to take advice from his officers. There were four cables running out of a little bay called Donigadee, all lying rather close together. In trying to secure the two ends of the damaged cable we somehow broke two of the other three cables because the Captain stubbornly refused our entreaties that he had overshot the cable track. By the time we had recovered and buoyed off the six cable ends the sea was awash with buoys. The Captain still would not accept any advice and recovered the wrong buoys. I was called to the test room where our Polish Captain was having great difficulty understanding the irate Irish gentleman on the radiotelephone who was apprising him of the fact that he had just connected Northern Ireland back to itself.

In frustration the Captain decided to send Mike (then cable officer) ashore in the launch, a heavy wooden boat of about sixteen feet, to sort out the problem at the repeater station on the beach. Taking two seamen with him Mike motored the one and a half miles to the shore only to discover that they were very low on fuel. Leaving the two jolly jack tars to get fuel Mike proceeded to the repeater station. Finding the station heavily fortified with sand bags and barbed wire (this was at the height of the troubles in Northern Ireland) it took him some time to gain access and to confirm that we had indeed joined up the wrong cable ends. On returning to the boat he discovered two very drunk seamen, an empty whisky bottle and no fuel.

Spying the returning boat party through binoculars, it appeared that Mike was rowing, with the two crew members slumped together in the stern. By the time he made it back to the ship Mike was not only exhausted but had huge blisters on both hands and buttocks.

That little old *Iris* and her sister ship the *Ariel* were often seen scuttling along the South Coast to repair cables around the UK coast. They were more that thirty years old, a good age for a ship, and their triple expansion steam engines were tired. I recall one occasion hearing on the radio a vessel reporting to Portland Coast Guard that there was a ship making heavy smoke out in the English Channel. 'Don't worry,' came the reply. 'Its just one of the Post Office Cable Ships in a hurry to get home for the week-end.'

I was once again back on the *Alert*, this time as acting captain, when the Spanish built their first cable ship. We were chosen to train the new Spanish Captain and Senior Officers. They struggled to absorb all the detail and unfamiliar tasks that covered our work but were in high spirits at the opportunity to have a fine new ship. When their ship was completed and they were given their first repair to undertake in deep water near the Equator, I was asked to accompany them, and flying out to Santa Cruz, Tenerife, I joined them by boat. I was met at the gun-port door by the Chief Officer, whom I knew well, and he accompanied me to the Senior Officers' bar. Raul the Captain was delighted to see me and as the sun was over the yardarm offered me a drink. The barman, with a big grin on his face, said 'Your usual sir, gin and tonic?' Somewhat taken aback I then recognised him from my days as a cable owners' representative on the Cable & Wireless ship *Cable Venture*, laying a cable in the Red Sea. It is truly remarkable what a close-knit community the Submarine Cable Industry is.

The repair went very well and I think I was able to help them through what must have been a very daunting repair. However there was an underlying aggravation of lack of unity between the Senior Officers aboard the ship. There was a constant battle for overall command of the operation. The cable engineering department and the ship did not operate as one and there was constant friction between departments.

The cable fault was in one of the repeaters (amplifiers) that in this cable were spaced about every twelve miles apart. As the cable was lying in a depth of two and a half miles, to get the cable to the surface requires the cable to first be cut and then each side of the cut brought to the surface separately. Not having the sophisticated hydraulic cutting grapnel that the *Alert* had meant that this was a long slow operation. To pay out the grapnel and rope to at least four miles is a painful operation. Paying out and picking up at about one knot each grapnel drive would take at least twelve hours and there were three drives at least.

In order to join the cable up again, the cable section had to be increased by at least twice the depth of water. This extra five miles of cable would unbalance the system and a mini system consisting of two repeaters and an additional twelve-mile section of cable was prepared. Once the faulty repeater had been removed the mini system was jointed in and laid out in a big zigzag to accommodate the slack. In this depth of water, clear from any trawler activity, the cable was not armoured, and whilst paying out the cable the outer polyethylene sheath touched on a rough protrusion somewhere on the hull. This filleted the cable, rendering it inoperative. Unfortunately the damage was not seen until some seven miles of cable had been written off. This was a very costly mistake but there was no alternative but to recover the damaged section and replace it.

All in all I think that the Spanish ship's first repair had gone well but it had proved what a highly specialist and sophisticated type of work cable laying and repairing had become. With the right tools and highly trained staff a very difficult task is made to look easy. The overriding lesson to be learned was the need for teamwork and unity.

6

CS *IRIS* GOES TO WAR

It was a cold December morning in 1975 as I stood on the banks of the river Tay and watched as the funny little red painted ship slid down the building ways and into the river. Little was I to know then how that little ship, just named that morning as CS *Iris*, would years later carry me to such remote and interesting places as Bahrain, Bombay, Hong Kong, Korea, Seattle and The Falkland Islands, to name but a few. She was probably the last ship built at the Rob Calledon shipyard in Dundee, who had a fine reputation for building good seaworthy vessels. I was there in the rank of Navigating Officer to assist in the commissioning of her sister ship the CS *Monarch* that was nearing completion and ready to embark on her maiden voyage.

The name Iris had affiliations with submarine cables dating as far back as 1855, when a navy hulk of that name helped in transporting cable from the factory at Erith down the Thames to the Brunel's flagship *Great Eastern* moored at Sheerness. This massive ship, a great triumph to Brunel's vision and engineering, was too big to get up the river. She was however the only ship afloat big enough to carry the thousands of miles of submarine telegraph cable to span the North Atlantic and thus connect Europe and North America. This link across the ocean was the first of many cables from telegraph to telephone, analogue to optical fibre, connecting the continents.

Such was the rapid advance in cable technology, that this first transatlantic cable was installed only a couple of years after the first submarine cable of any significance had been laid across the 22 miles of the Dover Straits. That cable, made from a strand of copper covered in rubber, or gutta percha to be precise, had been loaded onto a huge drum and laid from the deck of the tug *Goliath*. Once the cable was laid the English Prime Minister and French President sent congratulatory messages down this new exciting communications link. Unfortunately the link only lasted a few hours before the connection was lost.

Two days later a heavily laden fishing boat arrived in Ostend amidst great excitement. They had discovered mile upon mile of gold-filled seaweed!

There was clearly a need to give the fragile cable a protective armouring of steel wire.

I doubt if many people today realise as they sit at their computers, that their internet surfing is utilising optical fibre links through undersea cables spanning the world's oceans, and that this all began more than 150 years ago with a single strand of copper connecting two morse keys.

This *Iris* was designed specifically to operate in the North Sea and Home Waters as a repair vessel for the Marine Division of The British Post Office. With a length of 97 metres and a designed top speed of 14 knots she was equipped with a versatile combination of propulsion systems that would give her excellent manoeuvrability and station keeping. She was unconventional in shape, initially intended to be loaded with cable stored in large round containers lifted through big hatches and placed into the cable tanks in the bowels of the ship. Unfortunately this system was never used as it required the deployment of a floating crane and the removal of numerous of the hatches through the various deck levels. The whole process was far too lengthy and we returned to the time honoured method of pulling the cable in and out of the ship metre by metre, coiling it by hand into the tanks.

It was some six and a half years after that winter's morning of 1975 before I would sail on this little ship. I was standing once again on a foreshore watching ships pass out to sea. It was May of 1982 and I was standing with a huge crowd as we watched the pride of the British Navy sail out from Portsmouth to defend our sovereign territories in the South Atlantic. As Admiral Woodward's flagship HMS *Hermes* passed out through The Narrows she sounded *dit-dit-dit-da* on her whistle. With tears of pride running down my cheeks I wondered how many other people gathered there on the shore realised the significance of this Churchillian signal. The Old Man would have been impressed.

I was on leave having just left CS *Monarch* at annual refit on the Tyne, and was waiting to join CS *Iris* as Chief Officer. The weather was magnificent and I had just taken ownership of a little 23-foot wooden sloop. Built by Hampers of Fareham, renowned for building fine X boats, she looked like a cruising version of that popular little day boat. Drawing only 3 feet and fitted with a galley and four berths she was perfect for those waters. For two weeks I sailed her from her moorings in the Keyhaven River to all the little creeks and harbours around the Solent. I had just returned from one such idyllic day's sailing, calling in for lunch at the Bugle Inn in Yarmouth, when I received a message from our operations manager to tell me that *Iris* had been requisitioned by the Navy to assist in the Falklands Campaign and would I be volunteering my services. Without even giving it a second thought I said of course I would go. It wasn't until a couple of hours later, whilst eating my dinner, that the reality came home to me that I was going to war.

I was to join *Iris* in Devonport later that week, and busied myself making all the necessary preparations for such a monumental voyage. Not least of all I needed to arrange for someone to keep an eye on my pretty little boat whilst I was away.

As I walked through the naval dockyard at Devonport I was alarmed to see the changes that had been made to *Iris*. A large new helicopter deck overhung her stern and orliken guns had been installed on either side of the funnels. Knowing that she had very little cable on board I was concerned with the effect that these additions would have on her stability. As Chief Officer, stability was one of my responsibilities.

Having negotiated the gangway, where lines of sailors formed a chain loading truckloads of stores onto our little ship, I made my way down to the operations room deep in the bowels of the ship. There I was greeted by a very anxious naval architect. I had got to know Ray our naval architect over the years and had high respect for his opinion. His first words to me were 'I'm glad that it's you and not me going on this trip'. Not only had numerous structures been fitted to the upper decks but also several of the ship's water ballast tanks had been converted to carry fuel. 'If you get into the southern ocean and encounter any icing she will just bloody turn over . . .' were his parting words.

My first duty was to report to the Captain. Captain Fulton and I had been together for many years, both aboard ship and ashore, where we worked in the head office. We had a good understanding of each other's ways and made a good team. Whilst in the Captain's cabin I was introduced to our Senior Naval Officer (SNO) Lt Cmdr Bithell. He was to sail with us and was the interface between Merchant Navy and the Royal Navy. I took an instant liking to John and we were to form a close and lasting friendship.

We departed from Devonport, where amazing modifications had been made to our little ship in only three days. As we sailed past Plymouth Ho we were all very pensive, wondering what the next few months had in store for us. That night our orderly life was thrown into turmoil. A large rubber bag had been loaded onto the foredeck just below the bridge. It was contained by a steel bund measuring about 1 metre high and about 15 metres long by 8 metres wide. The bag, containing several hundred gallons of aviation fuel, was lashed down by webbing straps. As soon as the ship cleared the Lizard and rose to the, albeit very low,

Atlantic swell, this passive, benign slumbering giant turned into a crazed whale. The liquid surged fore and aft breaking all the straps and tried to climb out of the bund. Having been summoned from blissful sleep, together with half a dozen seamen I leaped onto this rubber roller coaster, trying desperately to pacify and restrain it. At times I was catapulted several feet into the air before the ship was brought onto a more suitable heading and speed was reduced. Eventually we harnessed The Beast but not before we were all severely bruised and soaked in aviation spirit. We were never to use this to supply aviation fuel but later emptied the bag into our own fuel tanks where it was mixed with diesel. The steel bund was cut up and dropped overboard.

The following day we rendezvoused with a RFA fleet Oiler to practise replenishment at sea. RAS-ing as it was called, was really scary. The other ship held course and speed and we closed in from astern. With the ships only about 45 metres apart we tried to keep station on her. A line was fired across to the Oiler from our foredeck. With visible tally marks hanging from it, this line was kept tight by hand to give us a guide to our spacing. The helmsman who never took his eyes off them said that he saw those tallies in his dreams for about a week afterwards!

Further lines were fired from amidships to which heavy lines were then attached. A short stumpy mast, called a RAS mast, had been fitted to our deck by the dockyard and a heavy purchase was attached between this and the end of the hawser. Tension was controlled by a dozen men hanging onto the end of the purchase; the rope paid in or out as required, to compensate for the lateral movement between the ships. Once the hawser was set up, a breeches buoy was attached to it and people, stores or fuel could be transferred from one ship to another via what to my mind was more like one of those extreme games invented by the Kiwis. I don't recall whether we actually transferred anyone that day but I certainly wasn't volunteering to be the guinea pig.

All this was conducted at a speed of about 11 knots and the tension on our bridge was electric throughout. The Navy Ships do this at double the speed and we were told that the faster the speed the easier it was to maintain the correct separation. Well, 11 knots was frightening enough for us thank you very much. The Captain later received a report from the Oiler and we scored marks of 2 out of 10. We did eventually get better at RAS-ing but it was never really our forte.

On our way south we called into Freetown for bunkers and fresh provisions. This gave our medical team a rare opportunity to practise their skills. The Doctor announced that every person on board had to be inoculated for at least six different things. They set up their tables in the ship's hospital and all hands were summoned to attend. I arrived there to find a most reluctant band of ruffty tuffty seamen trying to decide who should be the first to enter the torture chamber. Always having been a dreadful coward myself when it came to injections, I immediately felt all resolve melting away and my knees turning to jelly. There was only one thing to do and I stepped forward to lead the way. With the Doc standing on one side and the Medical Orderly the other and each brandishing a fistful of syringes, it was too late for me to turn back and before I realised it I was through and standing out on deck gulping down fresh air. Behind me was a very sorry sight as the others witnessed our cavalier medics practising their darts skills. I was so glad that I had gone first.

At Freetown with the help of our SNO, I had arranged for 100 tonnes of sand to be loaded into one of our cable tanks to help the stability crisis. This sand was dug up from a local beach and shovelled into hessian sacks on the quayside before being swayed onboard by crane. It was hot tedious work but I was much relieved at the improvement it gave to our stability.

We cleared out from Freetown and continued our way south. The following morning after a stroll on deck watching the silvery flying fish skimming the surface of the sea, I opened the door into the centre-castle to be met by clouds of flying insects. The sand had come alive and all manner of insects and marine life were hatching there in the hot confines of the cable tank. Fortunately my trusty Boatswain had gallons of Jeyes Fluid that we sprayed onto the sand and covered it over with heavy-duty plastic sheeting before tackling the clouds of flying insects. We were now all very glad that we had received those injections!

It was at this stage in our journey that we learned that our role was to be that of a logistical supply vessel, or LSV. We were to carry logistical supplies from Ascension Island to the various sections of the Task Force now deep in the Southern Ocean and around the Falkland Islands. We were one of four such vessels; the first two being HMS *Leeds Castle* and HMS *Dumbarton Castle* who were ahead of us, the fourth, the tiny *British Enterprise III* was to follow us.

We were exercised in various drills including the ubiquitous FOD-PLOD, a vital cleaning up exercise to remove any foreign objects, litter and anything unsecured that might be lying around the upper deck and could be sucked up by a helicopter.

On arrival at Ascension Island we were frustrated at the total lack of order and rationale of the stores being flown out to us by a fleet of helicopters. *Iris* was not built for easy loading of cargo and access from the heli-deck to the storage areas within the ship was via small stores hatches, narrow passages and doorways leading to staircases. This accumulation of stores on the flight deck was becoming chaotic. They ranged from helicopter engines and rotor blades to toilet rolls and photocopy paper, plus the hundreds of bags of mail destined for ships engaged in warfare several thousand miles south of us. They would be collected by helicopter and distributed around the fleet once we met up with them in the Southern Ocean. With no idea of order of discharge it was imperative that they be selectively stored below decks in an orderly fashion.

The SNO arranged for me to go ashore to help organise a loading sequence. As I arrived on the heli-deck that now looked reminiscent of a car boot sale, I was ushered forward by the FDO (Flight Deck Officer) who, placing a sling under my arms, gave the all clear to the pilot and I was whisked off the deck. Unknown to me Bith had spoken to the pilot and said, 'this is our Chief Officer who has never been in a chopper before. Give him a good ride,' The ship looked smaller and smaller as the helicopter rose into the sky with me suspended underneath by a thin wire. I don't know how high they took me but it felt like 2,000 feet before they wound me in and a strong pair of hands pulled me into the cabin. The pilot, high on adrenalin, proceeded to demonstrate his flying skills. I hadn't thought it possible to loop the loop in a chopper but he did it. Needless to say I was very relieved to reach the safety of the runway and put my feet on terra firma.

This wasn't to be our only eventful meeting with a helicopter at Ascension. We were informed that we were to carry some snow cats (armoured vehicles) for the Royal Marines. These were to be loaded onto the forward hatch recently occupied by the Av Gas bag. I requested that the helicopter transporting the cats to us use extended slings to ensure that the aircraft was well above the bridge structure. Regretfully my request was not heeded and a Chinook helicopter arrived with the first cat slung under it. I was standing on the bridge as the huge chopper descended to offload its cargo. The cat was level with the bridge windows when the throbbing of the chopper's rotors rose to a crescendo. The air pressure in the bridge started to pulse alarmingly. The snow cat suspended by a thin strap started to swing dangerously towards the windows. The Captain, SNO and I took rapid steps towards the back of the bridge and took shelter behind the chart table. We could hear things crashing onto the deck above and the SNO grabbed the radio and using very colourful language instructed the chopper pilot to abort the operation. Once relative normality was restored inspection of the Monkey Island showed that the 10 cm radar had been smashed to pieces with the motor and scanner scattered all over the deck together with several radio aerials. Apparently the oscillation created by the beat from the rotor blades had reached the critical harmony of bridge structure. The pilot of the Chinook later told us that looking down at the ship he saw the whole structure of the bridge wobbling like a jelly. Being no artificer in metals myself all I know is that it wasn't only the structure that turned to jelly on that bridge. Fortunately we were able to rectify most of the damage but the loss of our 10 cm radar was to prove very worrying later in the ice fields around South Georgia.

In addition to a most varied assembly of strategic stores and mail we embarked a detachment of Royal Marines. Originating from HMS *Endurance*, these guys had been landed on South Georgia to evaluate the situation when the Argentines invaded the island. After giving a good account of themselves by downing an enemy helicopter and sinking a submarine in the harbour, they were captured by the invading force and repatriated to the UK via Montevideo. They were now very anxious to return to their ship which was somewhere in the Southern Ocean. These guys were a really tough bunch. When offered bunks, they politely declined and rolled out their blankets on deck under the stars. I could understand why the Argentineans held them in such high respect. You don't mess with British Commandoes.

After two pretty hectic days at Ascension Island we weighed anchor and continued on our journey south. The first few days were in hot equatorial waters with smooth seas. Two days out from Ascension we had our first airdrop. We spotted the Hercules low on the horizon coming in fast. Stopping the ship we prepared our workboats for launching. The aircraft passed close up our Starboard side at an altitude of about 200 feet. We could see the ramp at the back open. She circled us once and then as she passed the bridge proceeded to drop five loads, each attached to a parachute. The two workboats bustled around recovering the parachutes and towing the loads back to the ship to be craned aboard. I can't recall what the packages, which measured about ten feet cube, contained but they must have been very urgent dispatches to warrant the expense of sending a Hercules all that way.

We drilled religiously and our naval contingent under the watchful eye of the Buffer, (the senior navy NCO), put us through our paces. I must say that we were at first pretty sloppy and the Buffer didn't hesitate to tell us so, but soon it dawned on us all that this was for real and that we were entering a serious war situation. The safety of our ship and our lives rested in our hands and if we were to come under attack there was nobody else to help us. Our drills became realistic when the SNO got the Chief Engineer to make a large gash in a 16 × 8 foot sheet of steel and the Buffer stood behind it directing a fire hose through the hole as we attempted to stuff the hole with wooden wedges and other materials. As he turned up the pressure what had started as a bit of fun playing with water in the tropics started to become serious. If you have ever been hit by the full force of a fire hose you will understand. I think it was when the SNO read us the Articles of War and we each received our identity disc that the true reality hit home. We were about to enter a war zone.

As we journeyed south towards our next destination, the lonely island of South Georgia, and started to feel the swell of the South Atlantic, our musters and drills took on a whole new aspect. From a casual five minutes at the outset we now had the ship closed up, with every man at his emergency station, in under twenty seconds.

We left the flying fish and dolphins behind and watched the grace of the albatrosses as they glided through the air on their huge wings. Could one of these birds really travel right around the Southern Ocean in 49 days? As the water got colder we saw more sea birds including Mother Cary's Chickens and our first sighting of a whale caused great interest. We received a signal advising that an Argentinean submarine was believed to be lurking in our area. Suddenly we all felt very defenceless. What were we doing on this little highly visible red painted ship with no naval protection except for two tiny orliken guns. Bith suggested to the Chief Engineer that we could deploy a Uni-foxer, (a decoy made up of jingling pieces of metal, towed astern to confuse the homing device of a torpedo). The Engineering department threw themselves into making the noisiest set of underwater organ pipes imaginable. I doubted somewhat the efficacy of this device. Surely we were sending out our calling card to any hostile vessel in the South Atlantic, but I guess it kept the guys busy.

Fortunately the following day we sighted ice. Submarines don't like operating in ice. I never thought that I would be glad to enter ice-studded waters but it gave us a strange sort of reassurance to be surrounded by icebergs. The next day we sighted South Georgia and in the afternoon entered the harbour of Gritviken where we found HMS *Endurance* lying to her anchor. As we sailed past her the Royal Marines were lined up on our flight deck carrying mops and buckets. It was quite a laugh to watch them go through their carefully rehearsed drill.

After an overnight stop, we left Gritviken and sailed around the coast to the old whaling-station of Stromness. This was where all the troubles had started a couple of months previously when a group of Argentinean scrap dealers had claimed South Georgia for Argentina. The place was amazing. This had been a hive of industry only a few decades before with full facilities to repair and refit whaling ships and their catchers. There was accommodation for over a hundred men and the mess huts were still laid out ready for the next meal. There were even bottles of HP sauce still on the tables. The stores contained everything needed to support this community and the engineering sheds were very impressive with blacksmith's lofts for bending huge pieces of metal into frames for ships hulls. It was apparent that when whaling stopped in the 1960s the whole place was abandoned and the entire community evacuated. There were ship's fittings of all shapes and sizes like anchors, propellers and mooring bits. People who had arrived before us had opened boxes and crates in search of booty. There were boxed sets of lignum vitae. This beautiful wood as hard as steel and self-lubricating was used to line stern glands. I picked up two small strips that Frank later turned into fids (wooden marlin spikes) for me. I still use them today when splicing rope, their exceptionally smooth, slippery surface making it easy to slide between the strands.

We had been given a shopping list of materials needed by the Repair fleet that was ready to patch up damaged ships from the British Task Force somewhere off the Falkland Islands. The DSV *Stena Seaspread* spearheaded this little repair fleet and we were to transfer these vitally needed stores at sea. There were dozens of gas bottles, bundles of steel, copper and brass bars and angles together with numerous sheets of heavy steel measuring about 8 × 16 feet. Before we could start loading we had to repair the wooden jetty, which had suffered storm damage. We were able to strengthen the structure sufficiently to support railway lines, which carried a bogie, ideal for transporting the heavy steel sheets and bottles from the stores to the ship.

With the combined efforts of the ship's crew and the navy contingent we completed our task and departed from this strange ghost town. Just outside the inlet we encountered HMS *Leeds Castle* and accompanied her back to Gritviken where there was quite a little fleet gathering. Six converted trawlers intended for mine sweeping duties had arrived. Then we learned of the eminent arrival of the *QE2* carrying thousands of troops ready to reinforce the invasion forces on Falklands. They were to be transferred to the *Camberra* and *Norland* as the *QE2* was considered too high a risk to go any closer to the action. As we could not assist in the transfer we were dispatched and sent on our way to rendezvous with the Task Force.

We received instructions that as we were approaching hostile waters we must not use our 3 cm radar as enemy aircraft could detect this. Having lost our 10 cm radar from friendly fire at Ascension Island, we were now devoid of any radar surveillance. We exhibited no navigation lights and the duties of the lookout had become of significant importance. As we steamed westward towards the Falklands we heard the tragic news of the sinking of the *Atlantic Conveyor*. The morale took a bit of a knock as we all realised the severity of our situation, and I think we all slept fully clothed for the next few nights.

The first that we knew we were nearing the fleet was the arrival of our first helicopter, and within minutes there was a line of choppers forming up astern of us. Word had got out that the mail boat had arrived and they were all desperate for letters from home. We were told to join the battle group and take up station astern of one of the carriers. We were later to discover that this was the position recently vacated by *Atlantic Conveyor*! This would be extremely dangerous in the event of an air attack as the Carrier would most likely deploy chaff to confuse incoming missiles and we would become her decoy. It was about this time that we had our first red alert. All those hours of drilling paid off as the crew went to emergency stations. I was stationed in the fore part of the ship with my damage control party and I reported all closed up in less than 90 seconds. We sat waiting not knowing what was happening outside and I think quite a few prayers were being said quietly. Suddenly over the intercom came the voice of Bith our SNO. To everyone's amazement he started recounting a story about the sexual life of the American male. The story just went on and on until finally he gave us the punch line and said, 'Oh by the way, the emergency is now over and you may all stand down.' Later over a pint in the bar he told me that he was scared stiff standing on the bridge but suddenly realised that most of us were in a far worse situation below decks and not knowing what was happening. It was certainly a very clever stroke and showed a brilliant understanding of other people's feelings in times of stress.

We were struggling to keep up with the fleet, as our top speed was only 13 knots, and we were not sorry when the flagship told us to peel off and complete our stores transfer with the *Fort Austin*. Once this was completed we were ordered to rendezvous with the repair fleet.

As we approached *Seaspread* it became obvious that to transfer our cargo wasn't going to be at all easy. The initial plan was to use the deep-sea tug *Irishman* to ferry the steel and bottles between *Iris* and the mother ship but with an enormous swell running there was no way that we could get close enough. After so much effort in getting the much-needed steel so far I was determined that there had to be a way to achieve our transfer. I discussed my plan with the Captain and Bith who passed the idea to the RN Captain E (the Senior Naval Engineering Officer) on the *Seaspread*. The Navy were only too delighted to stand back and let the merchant navy put our seamanship skills into practice. Using our buoy recovery gear on the starboard shoulder, I connected a composite steel rope to *Seaspread*'s after crane wire, forming a union-purchase. Using our forward crane, we hung off the first load of steel below the buoy skids and shackled it to the union-purchase rig. Lowering the load with our buoy gear, *Seaspread* took up on her crane wire. The water acted as a damper and *Seaspread*'s crane recovered the load onto her after deck. The first load took about twenty minutes to complete but the lads soon had this down to a few minutes. The ships had to be a matter of about 40 feet apart to successfully achieve our task and it was a fantastic piece of ship handling by both ships. The situation was made more difficult by the onset of night and the fact that we were unable to use deck lights for fear of detection by enemy aircraft.

As I stood on *Iris*'s foredeck I was at one moment looking down into her after deck and the next looking up at her rudder as the two ships moved up and down on that huge swell. At the same time as we were transferring our cargo on *Seaspread*'s port side a damaged frigate lay on her starboard side undergoing emergency repairs. One of our sheets of steel was lowered between the two ships and literally stapled in place to cover a huge gaping hole sustained from a missile attack in San Carlos Water. Those guys were doing a fantastic job in grim conditions.

By about two in the morning we had completed our transfer and everyone was relieved to say farewell to *Seaspread* and her flotilla of tugs. Little did I know then that many years later I should be in command of *Seaspread* in a later role as a Cable Ship stationed in Victoria, Vancouver Island. She certainly had a very varied and unusual history.

Our next liaison was with the hospital fleet consisting of the SS *Uganda* and some Navy survey ships. They too were anxious to get their mail. I guess that the sight of our little red ship bobbing up over the horizon made us very popular with all these ships staffed by such an unusual mix of civilian and military personnel.

Soon we were on our way heading back to South Georgia. The weather turned against us and as we approached the island we were nosing into the sea and taking heavy spray on the foredeck. On the *Iris* you couldn't see the foredeck from the bridge and as I went forward to prepare for entering harbour I was shocked to discover that the deck, structure and all fittings were covered in about six inches of ice. The words of the Naval Architect back in Devonport came back to me and I wondered how the weight of the ice was affecting our stability. Not having the luxury of steam hoses on a motor ship we had to resort to using buckets of hot brine to defreeze the capstans so that we could clear away the anchors. I was reminded of the whaling station at Stromness and what life must have been like on those whale catchers working in freezing temperatures with ice forming all over the superstructures and the rigging. It wasn't surprising that they needed such an engineering base on South Georgia.

After a short stop at Gritviken we resumed our voyage back to Ascension. We sailed east for several hundred miles before eventually heading north. That easterly course took us through heavy concentrations of icebergs. We doubled bridge watches and I split the night with the Captain. Fortunately we had our 3 cm radar back on although not the 10 cm which would have been very useful in these conditions. At one time I counted 60 bergs on the radar screen. I thought of the *Titanic*, and of the *QE2* who had sailed through these waters only a couple of weeks before and I wondered what the atmosphere must have been like on her bridge. Had they too had visions of Titanic in their minds?

Daylight found us still navigating in ice and the SNO decided that it would be a good idea to exercise the orliken guns. There had been problems with the shells jamming in the magazines due to age and a lack of grease. The nearest berg was selected for target practice and the whole ship's company were on deck to witness this exercise. No sooner had the gunners sent off their first salvoes than little black figures appeared all over the berg. To our surprise it was home to hundreds of roosting penguins who took great umbrage at being used for target practice. The exercise was suspended immediately and we left the penguins to get back to their egg hatching or whatever.

Communications with home were heavily restricted and we were all asked to contribute to a communal telegram. The message had to encompass the whole complement of both navy and civilian and there were many suggestions. The Captain gave the task of producing a united message to Bith and I. We spent some time sifting through the imaginative collection of ideas. The resultant text was put out for general approval and transmitted home. We heard later that it was well received by all. In fact unbeknown to us BT Marine had set up an excellent communications network with the families. This proved to be very effective and drawing them together in this way gave many of the wives and families tremendous support in such worrying and stressful times.

News gram received from CS *Iris* on 16th June 1982

> After the initial burst of activity on departing UK, the passage south passed quickly with numerous drills and instruction to equip us for our new role. Reception in Freetown was disappointing compared to Canberra's. Not a taut T-shirt in sight and no shore leave.
>
> C S *Iris* now bears no resemblance to a cable ship with many M.O.D.ifications, many resulting from Herculean tasks performed by own ship's company, to equip us better for our ever changing roles. At times we have been in company with many old friends, although under circumstances very different to a Spithead Review. Social evenings, when operations permit, have been enjoyed by all, to the benefit of the Guide-dog Fund. (We can now afford the lead!!!)

The crossing the line spectacular resulted in everyone in the pool. All hands are fit and well, thanks to Doc's hypodermic and Paludrin (anti-malarial tablets) – over 4,000 devoured so far.

We were pleased to have the company of some well decorated heroes for several days, and have made numerous new friends when arriving as postman flying our new Busby flag. He may lick stamps but we wish he would fly our way more often. Our own mail has proved haphazard and unreliable in both directions, but very welcome when it eventually arrives.

The camera buffs have had it good, shots of albatross, penguins and icebergs!!! Plenty of glacier mints but no polar bears or foxes.

MN and RN are now all one company and CS *Iris* now stands for 'Can Supply In Rain Ice or Storm'.

To date we have completed 110 helicopter operations, involving five types of helicopter (one 'by appointment'), one air drop of eight loads and eight ship-to-ship transfers, steamed 12,334 miles, peeled 33,000 potatoes, cracked 4,875 eggs and baked 6,000 bread rolls.

Our motto as always – 'Stay Flexible.'

Love All

The difficult access from our heli-deck to the ship's storage areas was still giving me concerns and as we travelled north towards Ascension Is. As the weather improved I drew up plans to hopefully remedy our problem. By removing the bow hoist, its carrier beam and the bow gantry we could create a well deck for'd where helicopters could easily deposit their loads. These loads would then be lifted by our forward crane and lowered through the forward hatch. By repositioning the beam and hoist in the upper working deck we could redistribute the loads within the area. This would also give us two helicopter working positions.

I put the idea to the Captain and SNO who both agreed. As we approached the doldrums with calm waters, we started to put my plan into action. The hoist itself weighed about 300 kg whilst the beam must have been nearly 500 kg. The lads did a wonderful job and we had the new transporter in place within a couple of hours. We had to wait until Ascension to get a helicopter to lift off the gantry of course but we all felt that we were now far better equipped to fulfil our new role.

It was at about this stage in our voyage that the Chief Steward discovered that a large number of sacks of potatoes were rotten. They had been supplied by an unscrupulous ship chandler in Devonport. Even more worrying was the find that about two hundred cases of beer were past their sell-by date. The Doctor condemned the beer and the cases were consigned to Davy Jones's locker, or so we thought. As I stood on deck with the Doctor the Bosun's Mate stood at the ship's side dropping the cases over the side. What we couldn't see was the other Bosun's Mate on the deck below catching the cases and passing them down to be secreted away. It was rather like small boys scrumping apples. The forbidden fruit always tastes nicer.

On 14 June we heard the exhilarating news of the Argentinean surrender in Port Stanley, and then seven days later the news of the birth of a son to HRH Princess Diana prompted a signal from the Admiralty to '*Splice The Mainbrace*'. Frank's skills were once again put to the test as he turned up two beautiful tot measures for the ceremonial dispensing of the rum tots. The ship's company was mustered on the helicopter deck and duly drank to the happy occasion.

A couple of days later we arrived at the anchorage off Ascension ready to start loading for our second round robin of the South Atlantic. Standing on deck I was looking at the desolate coastline when I was joined by Frank, who was puzzled as to the derivation of 'Green Mountain' on the far side of the island. Determined to find out I managed to arrange for the two of us to get ashore in the newly requisitioned sea rider, complete with its lovely big diesel outboard engine. Well after all, it had to be tested as fit for purpose!

Once ashore at Georgetown we managed to get a lift in a navy Land Rover up to Two Boats Village and then onwards up the torturous zigzag road up to the farm on Green Mountain. The Island is of volcanic origin, the last eruption being some 600 years ago. The land is mainly arid basalt lava and resembles the surface of the moon so much that it was used by the Americans to trial the Apollo moon buggy. It had been colonised by the British back in Napoleonic times and designated 'HMS Ascension' a 'stone sloop of war of the smaller class'. There had been a small Royal Marine garrison here since 1823.

The driver particularly liked showing off his skills by breaking and skidding the rear end to get around each hairpin bend. He dropped us by a stone archway that led into a pretty garden. There was a sprinkling of trees and under their shade in about half an acre of tilled earth were turnips, parsnips and other young vegetables for the local population. There was a small pub with the very British name of Red Lion, where we were able to purchase lemonade. We were directed to the entrance of a tunnel in the side of the hill. Above the entrance was the inscription *'Sic itur ad astra. Anno Domini 23 July 1832.' 'Such is the road to the stars!'*

Somewhat apprehensively we entered the tunnel holding on to a guide rope and inched our way into the darkness. The tunnel was barely six feet high and three feet wide and after about 100 yards it took a bend and we were able to see daylight in the distance. As we emerged from the tunnel we were astounded to step out into a totally different world.

Author sailing his firefly at Christchurch

23-footer from Hampers

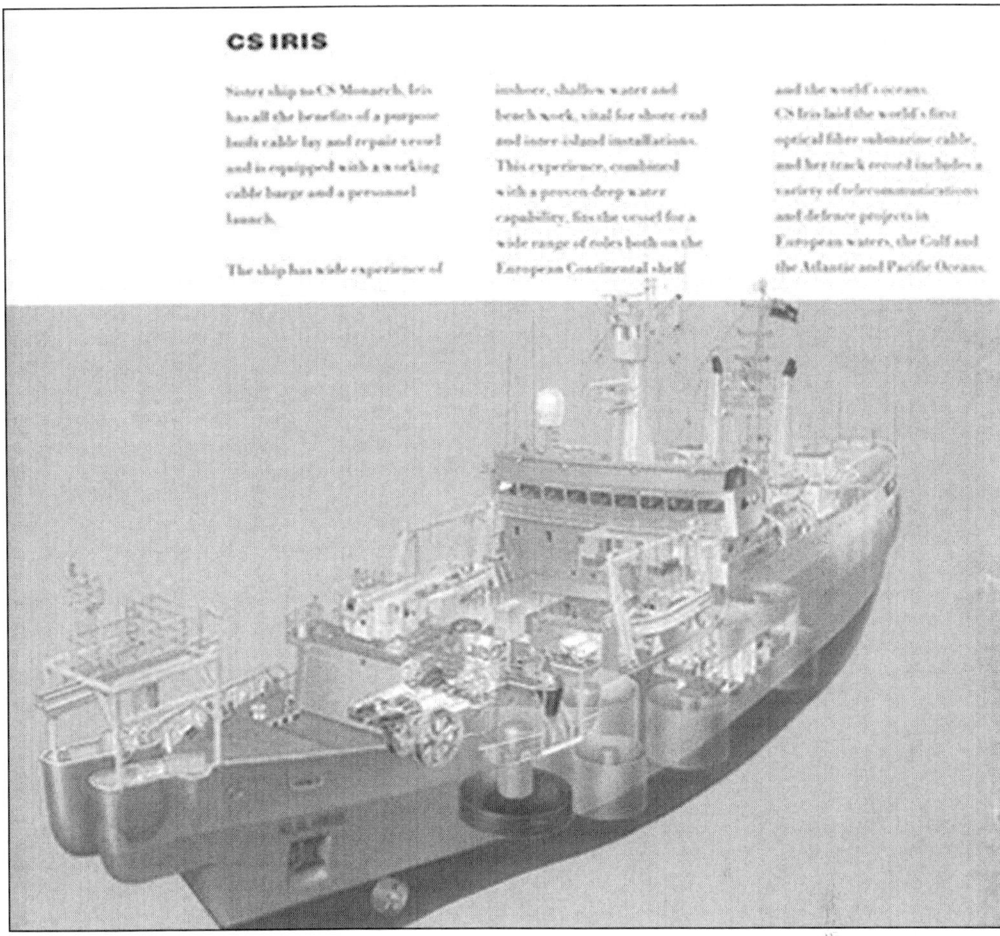
CS IRIS

Sister ship to CS Monarch, Iris has all the benefits of a purpose built cable lay and repair vessel and is equipped with a working cable barge and a personnel launch.

The ship has wide experience of inshore, shallow water and beach work, vital for shore-end and inter-island installations. This experience, combined with a proven deep water capability, fits the vessel for a wide range of roles both on the European Continental shelf and the world's oceans.

CS Iris laid the world's first optical fibre submarine cable, and her track record includes a variety of telecommunications and defence projects in European waters, the Gulf and the Atlantic and Pacific Oceans.

CS *Iris* in diagram

Helicopter ride

CS *Iris* at Stromness

CS *Iris* comes home from the Falklands

Captain

There was bird song and luxuriant vegetation. As a light misty rain fell around us, we took a path that led us up to a dewpond surrounded by groves of bamboo.

This side of the mountain, which faced the trade winds, was in total contrast to the hot burning desert of barren rocky moonscape we had left behind. Looking at this incredible sight I mused about the hidden treasures that these islands of the South Atlantic held, and gained some understanding of why we Brits held so dear the connections and fidelity of these island people to our own island existence. This was why we had mounted such a task force to travel tens of thousands of miles to protect our heritage.

We continued loading for our second run down to the Falklands, using our new helo dropping zone on the foredeck, which proved very successful, and we soon filled up all storage spaces. Whilst the war was in progress the MOD had taken many restrictions off the supply of stores, and ships were able to order carte blanche. The stores system consisted of computerised number coding which in general worked very well but occasionally a wrong number crept in resulting in the wrong item being dispatched. There was the case of toilet rolls for HMS *Coventry* where the Purser had ordered x number of packets instead of rolls. Each packet contained about a thousand rolls and had the Argentineans not sunk her, the weight of toilet rolls would have. As it was on *Iris* we did not have to order any toilet paper for years.

As we neared completion our helo deck was becoming very congested when the last load arrived by Chinook. It was a huge cradle which when landed took up most of the remaining space. As it was destined for the HMS *Invincible* with whom we were to meet up within a week it did not unduly worry me, but I would be glad to see it off the deck.

We were to carry a considerable number of passengers, who included clearance divers, various technical experts and a number of senior Naval Officers. Just as we were about to depart we were told that a contingent of six senior civil servants from the MOD would also be joining us. These guys were an advance party of technocrats sent to assess the damage and effectiveness of the Navy in real time. Accommodation was already stretched and these guys, all senior ranks, had to bunk up where-ever there was space. I converted the Ops Room into a six-man dormitory and any other vacant space was utilised. After their initial shock these guys all took on the spirit of *Iris* and we had some great social evenings despite our cramped conditions.

After visiting the depot tanker and taking on fuel we sailed south from Ascension into the warmth of the Doldrums. We had been instructed to rendezvous with *Invincible* and her escort group for our first delivery.

The guys were very pleased to see the *'Busby Ship'*, as we had become known, and the moment we appeared over the horizon a swarm of helicopters besieged us all wanting their mail. It was difficult preparing loads whilst we had this huge cradle on the after deck, but despite numerous pleas to remove it we hit a wall of indifference from all the choppers claiming various reasons why they couldn't take it.

I had been studying *Jane's Fighting Ships* to improve my ship recognition and on one occasion when visiting the bridge I noticed a ship approaching from the North. I announced to the assemble company that she was of the Bristol class. This produced laughter from the Navy guys, as there was only one Bristol, not a class. When Bith picked up his glasses he was surprised that I had been correct and in fact it was *Bristol* carrying the new Admiral who was to relieve Sandy Woodward. This caused great interest and things started hopping.

When a message from *Invincible* saying that they could not take the cradle until daylight the next morning came over the VHF my outburst of profanity caused by frustration was silenced by a very curt message. 'The cradle will be removed without further prevarication and *Iris* will proceed south at utmost despatch. FLAG.' The new Admiral had spoken.

Apparently the cradle was designed for removing a sonar bubble from underneath a ship's hull. This was a delicate operation usually conducted in port and to attempt this at sea in the middle of the South Atlantic was unbelievable. We learned later that the stores requisition had been wrongly compiled and they need a printed circuit board for the sonar not a cradle. I believe the cradle was later put into wet stowage or Davy Jones Locker.

When we arrived off the Falklands with the cessation of hostilities we were ordered to proceed directly into Port Stanley. The Army had taken over command of the STUFT ships (ships taken up from trade) and their organisation was chaotic to say the least. As *Iris* sailed into the sound every ship there watched with amazement at our approach course. The Army had failed to notify us of the existence of minefields laid across the entrance to the port by the Argentineans. In total ignorance we gaily sailed right through the area believed to be liberally covered by mines.

After Port Stanley we sailed around to San Carlos Water, which had seen some of the major losses sustained by the fleet. The weather was clear and bright and it seemed difficult to imagine such tragic losses had occurred here. The islands reminded me much of the Shetland Islands which explains why so many Falklanders are related to Shetland crofters.

We returned again to Port Stanley where we witnessed the tug *Irishman* towing the burned out remnants of the *Sir Tristram* into the port. As they passed us there was total silence as we all looked in horror at the result of the destruction of Bluff Cove. It was a chilling reminder of the enormity of war.

Later we collected the crew of the *Irishman* and took them back to Ascension for onward flights to the UK and leave. The *Iris*'s crew also were relieved in Ascension and soon after arrival we boarded flights to take us home. Whilst distributing mail around the fleet our own mail had been chaotic and it was only now that we received letters from home. Amongst my mail was a letter from my solicitor with a copy of my Decree Absolute.

Saying goodbye to Bith standing there on the desolate runway was difficult. We had been through so much together.

It was a long flight aboard an airforce VC10 where a few seats had been strapped down in what was primarily a cargo hold, but it didn't matter as we were going home. The catering on the flight was adequate, if not up to the standards of British Airways and several docking bottles (duty frees) were broached.

I was invited up on to the flight deck during the flight and then for our landing at Brize Norton I was privileged to get the jump seat behind the pilot. We were given instructions by radio to arrive outside the doors of the arrival area at a precise time and it hadn't occurred to me until then that we would be met by press cameras and families. Suddenly I was scared. I wished that I was back aboard *Iris* in the protective cloak that I had wrapped around myself. I knew that everybody else would have family waiting for them whilst I had just the grim reality of divorce to look forward to.

As we descended the steps from the aircraft on what was a beautiful English summer's day we were met by Bill Wainright our boss, who told me that my parents were waiting for me in the reception lounge. Thank God for Mum and Dad who were there when I needed them most. As I walked through the doors I was elated to see them standing there with my daughters Louise and Sarah. It was a very emotional homecoming.

CS *Iris* remained in the South Atlantic for another four months, making in all five round trips between Ascension and the Falklands. The original *Iris* crew returned in September. We were still doing our round robin between Port Stanley and Ascension and on our last trip south we were asked to call at St Helena, a lonely outpost in the South Atlantic whose inhabitants were suffering from the temporary loss of their ship, which had been seconded for duties in the Falklands. I had been asked to put a football team together and to arrange a reception for the Island dignitaries on board *Iris*. On arrival at the anchorage I went ashore to meet the Governor at his residence. Captain Fulton, a rather dour Scot, was not keen on entertaining and it had been left to me as Executive

Officer to organise such matters. The Governor, a charming man and a previous governor of the Falklands offered me the use of his car and chauffeur to look around this beautiful little island. All be it a whistle stop trip, it gave me a wonderful view of this delightful place.

I returned to the ship just in time to have my photograph taken with the football team who looked pretty formidable in home painted T-shirts and steel toe capped working boots. As trainer I gave them a lecture about being ambassadors and to treat the Islanders gently. No sooner had they departed from the gangway than we were told that the Governor's launch was approaching. Standing at the top of the gangway with Captain Fulton, he remarked on tropical uniform in the shape of empire length shorts not flattering his short and dumpy figure. With the soccer match still playing on my mind I introduced the Governor to 'Captain Football'!

As it was the football match was a white-wash, with the islanders winning 11-0. I think that this may have been partly to do with spectator harassment. There were supposedly eight women to every one man on the island (most of the men being away earning money for their families) and the pretty young girls around the touchline were too much of a distraction for the visiting team.

It was at the end of this last run to the Falklands that we were to bring the *Iris* home to Southampton in late November.

Once again we were advised that our arrival time was critical and we anchored off in Spithead overnight. At breakfast time I was surprised when the cross channel ferries coming out of Portsmouth altered course to sail close to us. The crowds of people on board were cheering as they passed the little old *Iris*. Surely they weren't cheering us were they?

Ships right through the port including *QE2* were dressed with flags and blew their whistles to salute us as we sailed up through the docks to our berth. There were helicopters in the sky overhead. We received such a tumultuous reception that included the band of the Royal Marines lined up on the quayside. We were all somewhat overawed by it all. We had only been doing what had been asked of us. I did feel so very proud to be part of CS *Iris* and her crew. They were a great bunch of lads.

Later I was to discover that nearly all the daily newspapers that day carried a full page picture of *Iris* with our motto ***C**an **S**upply **I**n **R**ain **I**ce **&** **S**torm.*

Twenty-five years later I am pleased to be able to recount the story of my first trip to the Falklands on our own little sloop of war, and I dedicate this to those who are unable to recount theirs.

7

TOTAL QUALITY MANAGEMENT

On the many occasions that I crossed the Bay of Biscay and rounded Cape Finisterre on the north western tip of Spain I had heard the fishing boats calling Vigo Radio but had no concept of how important Vigo was as a strategic base for the cable ships on stand-by covering the North Atlantic cables. Vigo was historically covered by a Cable & Wireless ship but occasionally one of the British Post Office ships was called to cover this station. Vigo has a very large natural harbour and history reminds us that as a base for the Spanish Navy it was frequently ransacked by Sir Francis Drake.

After our experiences in the South Atlantic *Iris* was called to cover Vigo in 1983. It was a popular station and we cultivated some good friendships there. One of these was a member of the Duran family who were our agents there. Ricky and I got on very well together and up until his untimely death in a road accident we had some good days sailing in his yacht in and around Vigo Bay.

It was whilst in Vigo that I extended my taste for Port. As Vigo is relatively close to the Portuguese border four of us hired a car and drove down to the border. Here we sampled some excellent food and discovered what a huge range of port wines there were. We were particularly enamoured with the white port that came in a wide range of tastes from very dry to very sweet. We purchased several cases covering a wide spectrum and headed off back to the ship. Sunday evening was traditionally steak night and now with the help of some excellent Stilton we extended our custom to include the very naval tradition of passing the port around the table.

Whilst very proud of their traditions seafarers are very conservative and generally dislike change but usually accept it begrudgingly. In 1991 we were introduced to Total Quality Management and to say that it changed my life is a massive understatement.

Jane was part of the team delivering the principles of TQM to the Company as a whole, including the ships. Businesslike marriage thrives on communication and that was what TQM was all about. The old concept that information was passed down on a need to know basis was replaced by open feedback in both directions. I, like many of my colleagues, was loath to accept the idea at first but needless to say I soon became swept up with Jane's enthusiasm.

Although I had to a large extent managed to conquer my speech impediment, standing up in front of a room full of people was still difficult and I could sit awaiting my ordeal in absolute agony. As I progressed upwards through the ranks the need for public speaking grew. With Jane's support and belief in me I gradually overcame my fears. Belief in myself and my subject was all important if I was to overcome my problem. The more I used the concept of TQM the more I grew to see its advantages and like the concept.

Shortly after the concept was introduced to us in BT Marine I was in Command of CS *Monarch* working up in the Hebrides. We had just finished a cable repair and were waiting to start a charter to the MOD to overhaul and repair seabed structures on their underwater listening ranges based at Rona in the Inner Hebrides. The *Monarch* had undertaken this work on a regular basis for several years although I had never been involved with it personally. As we had a day in hand before required on site I wanted to run through the work and what was expected of us. It soon became apparent that not only I but also none of the Deck Officers had any experience in this work.

I summoned all available staff together and asked for their thoughts and ideas on the tasks ahead of us.

Once we got started, the ideas came forth quite freely. I quickly built up a clear picture of the structures that had to be lifted and many of the pitfalls that had been encountered in the past. We certainly didn't want to make the same mistakes again.

There was the need for special stools to land the structures onto which the Chippy had made and were stowed in the fore hold. The Engine room POs told us about the unusual sheer bolts holding the feet of the structures, which broke away as the structure was lifted out of the muddy seabed and were then suspended by wire which could break without warning.

There was a need to have fire hoses rigged ready to wash-down these heavy beasts (some weighing as much as ten tons) as they came out of the water. The Chief Cook told us about the best and only place in the loch where we could safely anchor at night so that we could get television reception and mobile phone coverage (very important after a hard day's toil).

The cable jointing team volunteered to man the inflatable boat and jump onto the structure ready to secure lifting strops as it came clear of the water. All in all it was an extremely successful day and by the time we arrived on site the following morning I had a team who knew what they were doing and all necessary equipment ready and in place.

The work went extremely well and we finished well inside the allotted time. Our customer was very pleased and more than satisfied with our efforts which I know was the result of having a team who communicated well. The ship received a formal compliment from the Customer and an invitation to return the following year.

At one of our TQM workshops held shortly after the Rona work both Jane and I noted one of the seamen who had low esteem. When asked what his job was he said 'I'm just a seaman that's all. I don't know why I'm here'. He became a challenge to both of us and by the end of the session showed noticeable change. He had not long been with us and in his late thirties had been dealt some tough times in his life and had a clear lack of trust for authority.

Over the next few weeks I watched him change. I had asked him to become a mentor for a young seaman who had just joined us. Peter told me that he was determined that this young lad was not going to make the same mistakes he had made with his life, and this brought out a previously unseen side to his character. His whole appearance changed and he took on a fatherly role, which suited him. When I offered a prize for the best acronym formed from the letters of our ship's name CS *Monarch* it was Peter who came up with:

Customer Satisfaction Makes Our Name As Regards Cable Handling

Of course with this he scooped the first prize. TQM had certainly worked for Peter, who became a very loyal and trusted friend and a valued member of the team.

Never having been aboard a boat before meeting me, Jane very bravely agreed to join me on a cruise around the Channel Islands aboard my 26-foot boat which I had upgraded from the little wooden boat a couple of years before. We had some good fun anchoring in the little bays on such delightful places as Herm and Sark, and having explored Jersey and Guernsey we decided to try Chausey, the group of tiny French Islands to the south of Jersey. These islands have one of the highest ranges of tide in the world. We entered the sound at high water during the late afternoon and picked a spot where the chart showed we should remain afloat at low tide. The echo-sounder showed over thirty feet of water under the keel as I let go the anchor. Jane cooked us a lovely meal which was washed down with some nice French wine. It was a delightful place with hundreds of small islands and rocky outcrops surrounded by clear blue water.

All the day-trippers had returned to St Malo as we sat in the cockpit watching the sun go down before retiring for the night. It must have been about one in the morning when we were awakened by the sound of pots and pans falling out of the cupboard. The boat was listing heavily to port and Jane asked in a frightened voice 'What's happening? The world's turning over!' I tried to reassure her by saying, 'Don't worry. We have just taken the ground.' To which she replied, 'Well please put it back, I liked it the way it was.'

Hastily climbing out of bed I went on deck to investigate. The water had disappeared and we were high and dry. Not only was it spring tides but I hadn't taken account the high atmospheric pressure that was responsible for our fine sunny weather, but which pushed the water level down even further than the predicted level.

It was a beautiful clear night with a full moon (the reason for the spring tides of course) as I padded around the boat making sure that we hadn't landed on a rock, an anchor or anything that could have punctured the hull. Jane came out on deck to join me and we marvelled at the way the scenery had so dramatically changed from just a few hours before. The tide came racing back in as fast as it went out and within an hour we were afloat again and we returned to bed.

The following day we went ashore to visit the little café on the main island. By my watch it was twelve noon and the café was full of day-trippers. As the café stayed open until two o' clock we elected to go for a walk and return at one. On our return we were surprised to see the café empty, and as we entered the bar I realised yet another mistake on my part that, as we were now on French soil, there was an hour's time difference. Walking up to the bar and using my best schoolboy French I explained our predicament and that I was just a stupid Englishman who couldn't tell the time. With a very Gallic shrug of the shoulders he said it didn't matter and what did we want to eat. I suggested 'Fruits de Mer, pain et vin' which met with obvious approval. When the food arrived we were astounded. There was so much shellfish that he had needed to put it onto four plates. I think it was the best seafood I had ever tasted. Several people came into the bar and seeing our loaded table asked for similar, to which the barman said, 'No they are English,' which I suppose summed it all up.

After Chausey we sailed east to the pretty little port of Granville where I assured Jane we wouldn't go aground in the middle of the night. As there was no wind we motored across the sixteen or so miles, the water again was crystal clear and Jane was astounded at the huge number of jellyfish. After another delightful stay and two good nights' sleep we sailed on the rising tide, heading back to Jersey. We hadn't gone far however before the engine coughed and then came to a labouring stop. Looking over the side I could see the problem was a load of rope wrapped around our propeller.

As I stripped down to bathing trunks Jane asked what was I doing. I calmly said, 'I'm going over the side to cut the rope free'. With that she stripped off and saying 'if you think you are going into that cold water and having a heart attack, leaving me on this boat by myself, then think again.' As she jumped over the side realism hit her and she shouted 'Oh no those b***** jelly fish!'

Well, if this was Total Quality Management then I was all for it. It was during this trip that I proposed to Jane and she accepted, despite the jellyfish!

One example of when we needed better communication on *Monarch* was when the Chief Cable Officer decided to make some wooden flags. Whilst lying at our Depot berth in Southampton we were required to fly the hoist RY requesting passing vessels to go slowly. As a set of flags only lasted a few months the CCO decided in the interests of economy to make some from plywood. These were duly painted and hoisted. A few days later we received sailing orders and were ready to depart in the evening (winter time). As we were casting off from the berth the standby Quartermaster went onto the monkey island to lower the flags. In the wheelhouse we heard the shout followed by two very loud thumps. A very shaken and angry QM came onto the bridge saying 'What F***ing fool put those F***ing sheets of plywood up there. They nearly F***ing killed me.' The CCO looking very sheepish apologised most profusely. He had forgotten to tell the very people responsible for hoisting and lowering flags about his smart idea.

Ships are full of characters and Iver and Shiner were just that. Iver was very quick witted and always had a joke to tell whilst Shiner was solid and reliable. One morning half way through a particularly difficult repair I arrived on the bridge in the morning to a stony silence. OK, I said, what's happened? It was the duty Watch-keeping Officer who told me that the computer carrying the entire diary and positioning information about the repair had crashed. I replied 'Oh well, we still have the rough log, don't we?' Shamefacedly he said 'No, everything was on the computer.' Realising that my exploding wouldn't help recover the lost data I went in search of a hearty breakfast. It took the best computer brains on board six hours but eventually they managed to recover the missing information. The Navigator explained that he had allowed Iver to enter the data straight onto the computer to avoid duplication. Shiner not wanting to be left out had tried his hand. Now Shiner being a big chap had large hands and correspondingly large digits. Of course the inevitable had happened and he hit the wrong key.

When these two likely lads came on watch again at 6 p.m. I walked up to the helmsman, who happened to be Shiner, and casually said 'Now about the computer . . .' to which Iver suddenly found a need to leave by the back door. 'Have you a computer at home Shiner?'

'Yeh but me daughter won't let me use it cuz I f***d it up.'

'Would you like us to teach you how to use the computer, Shiner?'

'Is that before you f***ing sacks me or after?'

'Why should I sack you, Shiner?'

'Because I f***ed up your Computer.'

'Whose fault was it that the computer went wrong? Yours for not knowing how to operate it? Or mine for not making sure that people who had access to the computer had the necessary training?'

'Does that mean that it was your f***ing fault then, Skipper, when you wasn't even on the bridge?'

'That's what is meant by the buck stops here Shiner,' I said, and left them all to ponder on it. They always kept the rough log running after that lesson.

Two years after the Falklands escapade and several years before meeting Jane I decided to take my daughters on a sailing holiday in Cornwall. We had relations who owned a farm on the St Mawes River and they had agreed to put us up for a week. In anticipation of the holiday I had installed a 'Baby Blake' toilet for their convenience. First though I had to get the boat there and one glorious sunny week in early July I sailed her down to the West Country. With the promise of a good week's sailing I persuaded a lady friend to accompany me.

The first day was a leisurely run to Poole where we overnighted. We left the Town Quay and headed down Poole harbour, always a busy stretch of water. Rounding Old Harry Rock and then St Alban's Head we made good progress towards Weymouth when the Range Patrol launch came alongside to inform us that there was firing at the Lulworth Tank ranges and that we should stay at least four miles offshore. Thanking them for their information we sailed on with mackerel lines trailing astern hoping to catch our lunch. As midday approached we lost the wind. Seeing catspaws (tiny agitations on the water which resemble the marks of a cat's feet – the first indication of a breeze) on the water further inshore I headed closer in. The military were always over cautious, and besides the tank shells never really came out over the sea. With the sails drawing again we sailed on. Suddenly about fifty yards astern of us there was a huge splash. Surely they couldn't reach this far out? I was looking up at my lovely new mainsail and wondering what a shell shot would look like in it, when the second splash had me really worried. As casually as I could I started the engine and headed south at max speed. When the third splash came I was looking astern and hooted with laughter and relief as I saw a dolphin somersault in the air. Of course it had been attracted by the mackerel that were flapping merrily on the end of our lines. Throttling back on the engine I hauled in two lovely fish, which went straight into the pan to be served with new potatoes and garden peas.

Now why is it that some women always use half a roll of tissue when attending to the call of nature? Well, my crew on that trip was no exception, other than the fact that she used the blue industrial tissue that I used for clearing up fuel spills. On the toilet of a small boat, the discharge has to pass through a small seacock with a diameter of no more than two inches. As one can imagine the seacock can easily get blocked if excess tissue is used. Despite clear notices in the loo, the inevitable happened. Yes the toilet was well and truly blocked.

We put in to Weymouth for the night and once I had secured the boat to the pontoon, I set about clearing the blockage. This necessitated lifting the plinth that the toilet was mounted on and unfastening the flexible hoses connecting the bowl to the seacocks. With the whole assembly delicately balanced above my head I had just managed to remove the hose from the seacock when from the cockpit came a call. 'John there is a customs officer here who wants to see your logbook.' As politely as I could under the circumstances I suggested that she deal with it or ask him to come back later. 'But he wants it now' came the reply. Well he can't have it I shouted as I struggled with the connection. Just then 18 stone of Customs Officer stepped onto the side deck. The boat took a violent lurch and the blockage came free. Seawater jetted in through the open seacock and the bowl fell off its precarious perch. The entire contents of the pan emptied itself in my face. My face must have clearly showed my displeasure as I emerged from the forward cabin with bits of blue tissue in my hair. The Customs Officer had enough sense to beat a hasty retreat saying that he would return the next day.

It took us the best part of a week to reach the River Fall. I had been given a good safe mooring to use and I locked up the boat and travelled back to Christchurch by train. I had been really looking forward to spending a holiday with my daughters. Louise was fifteen and Sarah twelve, and Louise had brought a friend Karen along. I guess I had in my mind visions of how young people should spend their summer holidays from books that I had read as a child like *The Green Sailors* and *Swallows and Amazons*. I collected the girls and we drove down to Cornwall. The weather remained warm and sunny and we had a great time sailing around the River Fall during the day and staying at the farm overnight. We explored upriver up to King Harry Ferry where a couple of years before I had laid a cable across the river. There were some huge seagoing ships laid up, moored to buoys, including a couple of Blue Flue ships which I well remembered from my days in Liverpool.

There are several waterside pubs on the creeks around the Fall Estuary that we visited and the Helford River just outside the heads was our favourite. The farm was close to Saint Anthony's Head where the lighthouse had been used in the Children's TV programme Fraggle Rock. They were filming during our visit and the girls walked to the lighthouse to watch. One morning we had anchored close in to the lighthouse amongst the rocks. We wanted to explore the caves just under the lighthouse, and all piled into the rubber dinghy, and I rowed into the mouth of the largest cave. As we moved deeper into the cave the space became narrower and I shipped the oars and we pushed ourselves along with our hands. Suddenly there was a roar and a wave of water came towards us. With characteristic screams from the three girls we hurriedly backed out of the cave. They were convinced that a monster lay deep in the cave. Locals had told me that at least one of the caves went right through to join up with another cave, and this must have been our cave.

Whilst we sat getting our breath back Sarah said in a rather quiet voice, 'Don't move quickly because we are being watched'. There, only a couple of feet away, was a seal that had popped up to see what all the screaming was about. It had a pretty little face, rather like a young puppy, and it just sat there looking at us, showing no fear at all.

Returning to the boat I received another lesson in communication, or rather miscommunication. I had started the engine and shown the girls how to put it into gear before climbing onto the foredeck to weigh anchor. As the anchor came up I called to Louise to 'Come Ahead'. This was met with a mystified look and I repeated my instruction. 'OK Louise, Come Ahead'. Again there was no response, and by now the boat was beginning to drift towards the rocks. 'Louise, for God's Sake Come Ahead!'

Suddenly realising that the heads were in the bows of a boat, and using feminine logic, Louise climbed out of the cockpit and joined me on the foredeck. Fortunately it was Sarah (always the practical one) who sussed out the situation and put the gearshift into forward drive and taking hold of the tiller steered us out of danger.

It taught me a valuable lesson in how dangerous the use of jargon can be. We use so much jargon at sea and seldom stop to think whether the listener understands what we are saying. We glibly use words like deck, bulkheads, sheets, halyards, stays, fathoms and painters. I wonder what a non-seafaring woman would make of 'tighten up your backstay', or 'Grab hold of the painter', or perhaps 'we will slip her on the next tide', to mention just a few of our strange idioms.

It had been a wonderful holiday for all of us but I think that at the end of the week the girls had had enough of grumpy old dad and were glad to be going home to their ponies. I locked up the boat and leaving her in safe hands drove back to the New Forest.

8

BOMBAY REVISITED

When I left BI in 1970 I never thought that I would return to India, let alone Bombay. The little Cable Ship *Iris* built by the Post Office for repairs to cables around the inshore waters of the UK was never intended to be a world traveller, but she certainly was to take me to some interesting and far-flung places. I had just finished laying-up the *Iris* in Avonmouth docks as there was no work for her, when British Telecom Marine was sold to Cable and Wireless and our horizons were suddenly opened. The two fleets were to be amalgamated and staff united into the one company. I was the first senior officer to make the step across from one fleet to the other and was sent out to Singapore to take command of the Cable Ship *Venture*.

CS *Venture*, the largest ship in the C&W fleet, was in dry dock when I arrived and it was with hesitant steps that I approached the gangway, not knowing how I was going to be received. Fortunately I knew the ship well, having sailed on her a few years before as a representative for the cable owners on a cable lay in the Red Sea. I had been well treated on that occasion and had made some lasting friendships. My concerns were unnecessary, as, from the moment I stepped aboard, I was made truly welcome. It was a strange coincidence that the Cable Ship *Alert* was berthed at the next dock and giving both crews the opportunity to meet and intermingle. I think that my presence helped to give a kick-start to the process.

I knew that catering standards between the two companies varied greatly and that something had to be done pretty quickly or there would be a lot of dissatisfaction. When I had first joined the Post Office ships the catering was good but over the years with numerous economy drives the standard of food had seriously deteriorated. CS *Monarch* and the new CS *Sovereign* had contract catering and meals aboard those ships had become functional rather than a social event where people could relax and enjoy each other's company. The lifestyle of the two fleets was widely different. In 1974 the PO/BT fleet had moved to a new depot in Southampton and encouraged locally based crew. Whilst at their new base the ships would be put out of commission with all but duty staff going home in the evenings and at weekends. The Cable & Wireless ships on the other hand were stationed around the world and remained in commission at all times. Whilst BT employed all British crew C&W used mainly Filipino ratings and catering staff.

I arrived onboard *Venture* on a Sunday evening just as the Officers were finishing dinner. After welcoming me aboard we retired to the Officers' Bar and indulged in a few drinks to get acquainted. Word of my arrival had however reached the Cable Ship *Alert* and several of my old shipmates came aboard to see me. Well at least that was their stated intention, in truth I think that they had been waiting for an excuse for some while and I was the catalyst. We settled down to a pleasant evening although I was desperately tired from jet lag and a long flight. It didn't take the *Alert*'s lads long to find the menu from that evening's dinner. They were aghast at the difference to their meagre rations. Their evening meal had consisted of corned beef hash. In contrast the *Venture*'s menu looked more like that for a banquet.

On the following morning I asked the Third Mate, who was responsible for issuing working gear, for a boiler suit and pair of boots and I requested that the Chief Engineer give me a tour of the Engine Room and Dry Dock to inspect the ship's hull. The look of utter bewilderment followed by disbelief that came over the Chief's face was a picture. Why would anyone in their right mind go into a ship's engine room in the tropics if they didn't absolutely need to? The ship was in dry dock to replace a broken generator. The easiest way of doing this was to cut a big hole in the ship's side, take out the old generator and slide in a new one. The Chief, determined to see me sweat, gave me a very extensive tour and I returned to my cabin exhausted but with a clear understanding of the conditions that the engine room staff were toiling under. Several years later he told me just how much his staff had appreciated my consideration.

We soon left the dry dock and moved out to the eastern anchorage where we had some very pleasant days in the less humid and oppressive atmosphere. Being an old ship the air conditioning on *Venture* struggled to handle the Singapore temperatures but she was fitted with lovely old fashioned awnings which gave her a very elegant appearance and areas of deck ideally suited to deck sports and barbeques. I was to sample my first C&W barbecue, which was magnificent. There were grilled jumbo prawns the size of lobsters, tender Australian steak and fresh strawberries.

I thoroughly enjoyed my short time on the *Venture* and was reluctant to leave, but on my return to the UK, one month later, I was greeted with the news that *Iris* was to be recommissioned for a US Government charter. This was welcome news and when we sailed from Falmouth a few weeks later I was lucky to have my wife with me for the outward voyage. We sailed across to Portsmouth New England to load cable and then down the East Coast of The States, through Panama Canal and up the West Coast to Seattle. It was a marvellous opportunity for Jane, who saw the most amazing assortment of sea life including Whales, Sharks, Turtles and Seals.

We had some pretty heavy weather crossing the North Atlantic, which she took in her stride, and on the evening of the sixth day I told her that the following morning she would be in for a surprise. We were just approaching the Grand Banks where the warm water from the Gulf Stream meet the Cold Alaska Current, and providing we didn't get fog the sealife would be plentiful. Sure enough as we went onto the bridge the lookout sighted the first whale. Watching as they broke the surface of the sea and their great fan tails reached into the air was something she will never forget. The air was positively full of birds and our run from the edge of the Banks to Martha's Vineyard made up for the preceding week's bad weather.

While we loaded cable we were able to take in some sightseeing and we both enjoyed New England. We sailed from Portsmouth, New England bound for Seattle via the Panama Canal. Jane saw some magnificent scenery and even experienced the birth of a hurricane that formed around us as we headed up the West Coast. The weather was very odd that day with very heavy cumulo-nimbus cloud forming all around us. The water was relatively calm but fidgety. During the night we watched the most spectacular display of lightning, with the whole sky lighting up. The barometer was falling all the time and I was aware that we must be in the centre of a newly forming depression. I contacted the United States Hurricane Centre and sent them four-hourly reports. By breakfast time the next morning we were beginning to draw away from the centre and the wind and sea started to increase. I was fairly certain that as the depression was still in its infancy the eye would continue in a westerly direction, and making all possible speed we headed north west. This was not necessarily the best quadrant to be in but we had little option and I was very relieved that by the following day both wind and sea had moderated considerably. *Iris* is a very good sea ship and I have experienced some very rough conditions in her both in the Southern Ocean and the North Sea, but one doesn't play the fool with Tropical Revolving Storms.

On completion of our charter the *Iris* left San Francisco for Hong Kong, where we hoped that more work would become available for her. Over the next six months we picked up scraps of work until the South Korean Telecom Company chartered us for maintenance work on their domestic cables. They were a part of a syndicate of Cable Owners whose interests covered the Mid Pacific to Aden, although we did not expect at that time to go any further west than Hong Kong. *Iris* was in fact in Hong Kong when, on completion of some leave, I was summoned to Head Office for briefing.

We were to make a repair to one of the many cables running out from Hong Kong and then to my surprise make passage to Bombay, where a major cable had been damaged. Two other cable ships had been despatched to undertake this repair but neither had reached Bombay. The Cable Ship *Enterprise* freshly out from refit caught fire whilst still in the Malacca Strait and had returned to Singapore. The *Asian Restorer* also based at Singapore sustained steering gear problems in the Indian Ocean and was limping home to Singapore. I was advised that our customer the Indian Telecommunications Company VSNL were less than happy with the situation and I was to make best speed to Bombay, calling on route at Singapore for cable.

Flying out to Hong Kong I realised that we had a very diplomatic role to play, and I looked forward to returning to Bombay, nowadays known as Mumbai. The Hong Kong repair went well and three days later we were on our way down the South China Sea at best possible speed. As the *Asian Restorer* had taken most of the stock cable there was little left for us in the Singapore depot and I requested the other ship to stream the stock cable for us to pick up on our way west. Despite being assured that this would happen, for reasons best known to themselves they failed to stream any cable, and so we continued on our way to Mumbai.

Leaving the Singapore Straits just before midnight we received a stark reminder of how dangerous that busy stretch of water can be. Because of the huge volume of traffic, Singapore Traffic Scheme uses two VHF frequencies, One for East-going and one for West-going traffic. We were tuned to the West-bound channel but were also monitoring the Emergency Channel 16.

As we approached Raffles Light I saw two large images merged together on the radar screen. This would be quite natural as the Straits are at their narrowest at that point. I was however puzzled and then alarmed when the targets didn't separate. I reduced speed and posted additional lookouts. As we closed the alter course position off of the Light there was a huge concentration of shipping, with most ships still closing the area at full speed. There was the usual pathetic rubbish being generated on Channel 16, but retuning to the East-bound frequency I could hear the rescue services broadcasting information of a collision.

There were tugs and small fast rescue craft everywhere and we were clearly not required, and as other shipping was not reducing speed we would be exacerbating the situation rather than helping by hanging around. Having passed my position and intentions to Singapore Radio I reluctantly increased speed to get out of the congested area. It went against all my training to leave the area but we had been told that we were not required and it was clear that the emergency services had the matter under their control. As we passed Raffles Light I could see a vessel clearly sinking at the bows with her stern in the air. Her propeller was still turning while we just looked on helplessly.

That sight gave us all much to think about in the next few days as we crossed the Strait of Malacca and the Indian Ocean.

As we entered the harbour of Mumbai there was a deal of commotion with fishing vessels garlanded with flowers and flying huge flags dashing backwards and forwards. The sea appeared to be full of coconuts. The pilot explained that they were celebrating the end of the Monsoon and that the coconuts were a gift to the gods.

I had been advised at the briefing that two of our Company's ships had experienced bureaucratic difficulties in Bombay earlier that year and I prepared myself for some delicate diplomacy. On our arrival various representatives from the VSNL, the Indian Navy and Bombay Harbour Authorities came aboard together with our ship's agents. Trying desperately to remember my Hindustani I welcomed them all and we sat down to negotiate. To everyone's surprise, the small town of Jhansi in central India where my mother had been born was also the birth place of the young VSNL representative who was to accompany us on the repair. This put me in good stead and from then on I was known as Jhansi Walla. This together with my BI connections gave me good standing with the various authorities.

The following day whilst waiting for clearance to work in these waters I decided to visit the offices of VSNL and the other concerns. Although the monsoon was supposed to have ended there was torrential rain as we went ashore by launch and our umbrellas were of little use as Jim (My Chief Engineer and long term friend) and I arrived at Ballard Pier. We received a warm reception at the Agents' where I renewed some old links from my BI days. We were ushered in to meet Captain Couto the Managing Director who was held in very high esteem. He was a delightful old gentleman who had an abundance of amusing stories. He explained the significance of the coconuts that the local fishermen had thrown into the water. One tale was of a heavy vehicle that could not be moved up a steep ramp from a ferry. With the tide rising there was risk of losing both lorry and cargo. In desperation he took two coconuts and smashed them on the ramp. Miraculously the tyres suddenly got a grip and the vehicle climbed the ramp to safety. 'So you see young man (I was well into my fifties), never underestimate the venerable coconut!' was his parting remark.

My nick-name had preceded me at VSNL and a lot of people wanted to meet Jhansi Walla. Our third stop was at the Offices of the Harbour Master who was a very important man and one who could help me in many ways if he was on my side. We were hospitably received and I returned to my ship feeling that we had achieved a good PR exercise. All we had to do was to repair the cable.

It transpired that several large vessels at anchor off the port had dragged their anchors in a cyclone and had ripped several holes in the cable despite it having been buried. It appeared that my PR exercise had been successful as we were granted permission immediately to commence our work. Grappling for the cable soon showed me that the damage was extensive and that most of the cable along a distance of eleven kilometres had been badly mauled. Having established a good end to seaward this was sealed, anchored and buoyed off. I then started to work inshore. It was indeed fortunate that the monsoon was at an end and that there was little or no swell running. As we inched our way closer and closer towards the beach the depth of water was decreasing alarmingly. We finally recovered sound cable less than two kilometres from the beach with only two metres of water under the keel. With an eleven-kilometre gap in the cable and only five kilometres of stock cable we needed to cut out as much usable cable from the recovered cable. As we tried to turn the cable over from one tank to another sections of cable were so severely damaged that our cable-hauling machinery would not handle the torturous corkscrew.

Fibre optic cable is constructed with a number of strands of fibre individually wrapped and then parcelled together and encased in polyethylene and shrouded in a light wire sufficient to give linear strength to the package. Whilst fibre optic cable laid in deep ocean depths needs only light protection, in depths of less than two thousand metres it is given protection against trawling and anchors. This will range from light armouring to heavy and usually double armouring in areas of high risk. Most of the recovered cable was double armoured with two layers of twelve gauge galvanised wire and several layers of rope serving. Deep-sea cable will be only a few centimetres thick but heavily armoured cable can be as much as ten centimetres or more in diameter. To cause damage of this severity I estimated that the cable must have come under tension of thirty tons or more. To enable us to salvage sufficient cable to fill the gap I needed either a clear dock space or large barge to pull the cable onto. Returning to Mumbai I was relieved when the agents found us a very large barge with winches mounted at one end. This couldn't have been better and with the assistance of a couple of gangs of local labour we commenced the difficult task of cutting out and jointing the good lengths of cable together.

During our recovery exercise we had lifted a large anchor with the cable entwined in its flukes. We had managed to lift the anchor onto the foredeck, as VSNL wanted to use it as evidence of their legal case against the ship's owners for breaking the cable.

It took us days to haul all that cable out of the ship and to splice it together but eventually we had sufficient stock to complete the repair. We were now however into the cycle of spring tides that gave us even less water under the keel at the inshore position where I needed to make the initial splice. Conscious of the scrutiny we were under I could not afford any further delay and I returned once more to the cable ground, first checking on the buoys on the seaward end.

With a very close eye on the depth recorder we nosed in to recover the cable end and make our splice to the stock cable. This job was clearly fated as just as we started the satellite communications failed. Good continuous communication is essential during the jointing of optical fibre cable as numerous tests are made. We resorted to a mix of hand-held VHF sets and mobile telephones to assist us and it was with high adrenalin pulsing through me that I took the controls at the commencement of the lay-out to the other cable end eleven kilometres away. As we approached the area where we had buoyed off the cable end there was no sign of the buoy. The fishermen had clearly been unable to resist it and had cut it from its moorings. This meant that I had to lay out to the end of my stock cable, buoy that off, grapple for the moorings and recover the seaward cable end before recovering our stock end buoy and make our final splice. I was never so pleased as when I saw the bight of jointed cable disappear over the bow and lowered onto the seabed. We returned to the harbour to await clearance that the cable was fully functional once more.

We were very soon contacted by a very pleased representative from VSNL who told us that the cable was up and running with all fibres functioning correctly. I also received an invitation for lunch with the local directors of VSNL, which I gratefully accepted. Together with a selection of Officers I preceded ashore. Like most prestigious places in India the restaurant looked just as scruffy as the next from the outside but once through the outer door we entered into a different world. There were open air courtyards with trees, flowers and fountains. Even the birds whistling in the trees were different. We sat down to an amazing meal which we all thoroughly enjoyed. It could not have been further removed from what we in the western world think of Indian food. Our hosts were charming and gracious and we were continuously told how much our work had been appreciated. Our meal however was brought to a somewhat premature end by a telephone call from the ship. A fishing boat obviously in trouble and in danger of sinking had come alongside the barge which was still alongside *Iris*. There was great concern that if the fishing boat sank the *Iris* could swing and become entangle in the wreck. Whilst the harbour master was anxious that the boat remain alongside us until help arrived, I was acutely aware of the risk to *Iris*. The ship's crew had put several stout lines around the fishing vessel and were helping, with the aid of a portable pump, to reduce the water level in the boat. Suddenly help in the form of a number of other fishing boats arrived. With lightning action these friends had untied the sinking vessel and with our lines and pump still aboard made off with the vessel across the bay. Not only had the local fishing fraternity taken our buoys but they now had made off with a quantity of good rope and an expensive pump.

We still had to land the anchor that was proving to be another sticky problem. The high temperature and humidity was causing havoc with the hydraulics of our foredeck crane. Jim had ordered several new sets of hoses from a local engineering firm but as soon as we attempted to lift the heavy anchor the hoses would blow. I contacted VNCL and the agents to suggest that we land the anchor at Singapore, but their insistence to have the anchor in Mumbai gave me no alternative but to keep trying. As Tony the Second Engineer, bathed in sweat and covered in hydraulic fluid, fitted our last set of hoses, I had an idea. I raced up to the radio room to see Sparks, another ex-BI man. He had been ashore the previous night and had seen a load of coconuts literally fall off the back of a lorry. Knowing of my predilection towards coconuts he had recovered two to the safety of the ship.

Taking my prize up to the crane deck I placed them both on the anchor and told Tony to smash them. Uttering a great deal of profanity about the Old Man having lost the plot and didn't he have enough work to do without playing silly games, he finally obliged and picking up a sledge hammer smashed the shells to pulp. I instructed the crane driver to lift the anchor and with my heart thumping watched it lift and swung out over the side to a waiting barge. As we lowered the anchor onto the barge the deck of the wooden barge shattered and the heavy anchor went strait through into the hold beneath. There was a tremendous cheer from my crew as the weight came off the crane. To this day I still get reminders of the witchcraft I used in Bombay. The following telex received from Captain Couto said it all.

> FAXIMILE TRANSMITAL MESSAGE
> From Patvolk
> Mumbai
> India
> 17th September 1998
>
> Dear Capt NEWBURY
>
> We have been edified and enlightened by your fax dated 24th September contents of which were avidly read by my colleagues as well.
>
> Let me say what a great pleasure and wonderful experience it has been to work with you and your team and if it was not for the endearing cooperation and motivation we would never have been able to sustain quantitative customer satisfaction. We learn that VSNL are indeed happy with your performance and the subsequent delivery of the incriminating anchor and chain as a source of evidence to enable them to press their claims.
>
> Indeed glad to note the efficacy of the coconuts, a hoary tradition from the distant past to calm the seas and ward off adversities.
>
> Thank you for the warm sentiments expressed in your letter and your sentiments will definitely go a long way in promoting and strengthening our existing relationship and be assured of our reciprocation both in spirit and in deed.
>
> Hope fervently that we may have an opportunity for our paths to meet soon, in the meantime may you encounter favourable winds and following seas.
>
> Best regards
>
> Capt A.J. Couto

With the cable successfully back in service we were clear to depart for Singapore, although VSNL had made concerted efforts to have me remain there for a forthcoming meeting they were to have with Cable & Wireless Marine. There had been considerable interest in placing the *Iris* on stand-by in an Indian port to maintain their cable systems. I was extremely proud of my ship and crew for the way they had entered into the challenges that this repair had produced. It was with great pleasure that a few days later I received the following message from our Marketing Director.

> Extract from Rob D's visit note on return from meeting with VSNL 17th Sept;
>
> 'VSNL very pleased with recent completion of SEMEWE2 repair by CS *Iris*. Special praise should go to Capt John Newbury and his crew on the *Iris* for promoting CWM in positive light. This certainly made the meeting much easier for me and has positioned CWM well for the current opportunity with VSNL.
>
> I have heard of the trouble you went to and the successful completion of the repair and remedial work. The Chairman wishes to be sure that you are aware that we very much praise your efforts. Well done, many thanks and good wishes to you and all on board.'

As it was CS *Iris* was granted a very lucrative contract and placed on standby in the Indian port of Cochin the following year.

9

IRIS AND THE US ARMY

Much of the damage done to cables on the seabed is related to fishing activity. South Korea was no exception and the first repair that *Iris* had been required to undertake on her charter to South Korean Telecom was to a domestic cable running out to the Island of Cheju, known as the honeymoon island for its popularity with newlyweds. The area surrounding Cheju is heavily fished and is also affected by strong tides. The fishing vessels work in pairs with the net slung between them. They are fitted with special anchors with a single long fluke up to two metres in length. Once in position they deploy the anchors and drift down on the tide, dragging the anchors with them. The cables don't stand much of a chance and this cable was a frequent casualty. Whilst we were repairing the cable it sustained a second hit literally less than a mile away and we thus had two repairs to undertake.

That area is also worked by squid fishing boats. The Koreans will eat almost anything that comes from the sea. These boats are equipped with long booms from which are suspended numerous powerful lights. A large number of these boats will work together and the effect of all their lights together is quite remarkable. It reminded me of a huge firework display. They do in fact constitute a danger to navigation as approaching vessels have difficulty in making out the lights of other vessels positioned between themselves and this backdrop of concentrated illumination. We had several near misses from passing coastal traffic whilst making our repairs, as we lay hampered by the cable suspended from the bow and unable to take evasive action ourselves. It was also interesting that when on one occasion we sighted a large oil slick that we duly reported to the authorities they were totally uninterested and just didn't want to become involved. So much for IMCO regulations!

After the rather pleasant interlude of Mumbai I was not looking forward to returning to Pusan. In the six months since we had taken up the maintenance charter there, the agents had been unable to secure us a berth and we had been left in the harbour, swinging to the anchor. To get ashore we had to use ferryboats but as they finished work at 2100 hours it was very limiting on what people could do as it meant being back at the ferry by 2030 hours. When the weather turned bad, which was quite often, the ferry would just stop operating with no prior warning and our crewmembers would be marooned ashore.

It was here that I noticed the difference between the C&W and ex-BT staff. Most people who had joined BT cable ships had done so to be close to home most of the time. They did not like being on the other side of the world far from their families. On the other hand the attitude of the C&W lads was very Gallic and a case of 'Oh well we are here so let's make the best of it.'

We left Mumbai with just a passage crew. It had become uneconomical to keep a British crew (that is deck and engine room ratings and catering staff) whilst stationed on the other side of the world and we were to change at Singapore, picking up a Filipino crew before returning to Pusan. I was reluctant to see the Southampton lads go, as I had known many of them for twenty odd years, but realised the economic reasoning behind the move. This did make life a little easier as the Filipinos were far less demanding than their predecessors. I also wanted to use this change of crew to redress the catering mismatch and bring *Iris* up to the same level as the rest of the fleet.

I managed to secure a berth alongside for a couple of nights in Singapore and we had a farewell party to see the lads off. I had arranged for a gang of local labour to totally clean out the crew's accommodation and we were very surprised at the way the cleaners relished items which we considered to be rubbish, A part used bar of soap and a half empty aerosol can became prized possessions. I think that the recycling authorities in the UK today could learn a lot from these poor people.

I had never sailed with a Filipino crew before and I wanted to start off as I meant to continue. Having heard of some pretty despicable ways that some had been treated I was not having racist attitudes aboard my ship. As they were arriving in the evening I arranged that I together with Jim and the purser would meet them on arrival at their hotel. The purser gave each an envelope with a list of the Officers' names and a small advance of cash. Tito the Chief Cook, who appeared to be the self appointed leader, stepped forward and thanked us for our unexpected welcome. I was soon to find out what an asset I had in Tito. I learned later that he had been head chef in one of Manila's top hotels where he was highly thought of both afloat and ashore.

This little bit of consideration was quickly rewarded several fold as the new crew settled in and I saw the efficiency levels of *Iris* rise. The ship was cleaned from top down and pieces of equipment that hadn't worked for years were suddenly fixed. I soon learned how versatile and industrious these people were. Machinery that was unusual and specific to *Iris*, they quickly became accustomed to. My major concern now was how to ensure that the lads pay sufficient attention to safe working practices in their eagerness to oblige. As we dropped the Singapore pilot a rope became entangled with the pilot ladder. Nothing daunted one of the seamen climbed down the ladder to free it, oblivious to the fact that the ship was travelling at 13 knots through busy shipping and that he had no safety harness on. Obviously there was a strong need for safety lectures from the senior officers.

Once back on maintenance duties, we were called out on various local repairs and when returning to Pusan from one such trip just before Christmas, I was determined to find us a berth. My wife had announced that she would be travelling out to join me for the festive season and this made me all the more determined. I had a stinking cold and had gone ashore to the hospital. Before I could be treated I had to be issued with a hospital Identity Card (photograph and all). Having been given an injection I returned to the Agents' Office ready for battle over the berth. After a lot of sucking in of air between clenched teeth Mr Lee said it was impossible because like in Japan the Longshoremen's unions controlled the entire waterfront. As we were not loading or discharging cargo they would not allow us to monopolise a berth. With a chart of the harbour in my hand I looked out across the harbour from his office window and identified one berth that I had noted seldom had a vessel berthed alongside. This I was told was the United States Army berth. Pointing out that the US Army would have no truck with stroppy unions I demanded to be taken there whilst leaving the Purser to go to the bank and sort out other domestic business. I don't know what I had expected but I was becoming desperate in my quest for a new home for my ship.

When we arrived at the berth we were met by barbed wire fences and armed guards. I told the agent to explain who I was and that I needed to speak to the Officer in charge. The sentry demanded to see some identification and that was a problem as I had given the Purser my passport to go to the bank. Brandishing my bright new hospital ID card worked miracles and we were allowed through the gate and directed to some offices over a warehouse.

On approaching the offices an Army Officer who was so tall he should have been playing for the Harlem Globe Trotters and displaying various pips and other emblems on his shoulders said in a very Southern States drawl, 'Say, you guys look like you're lost, can I help?'

Drawing myself up to all of my five foot eight inches I looked up at this giant of a man and said. 'I am the captain of that little British ship anchored out in the harbour. We are far from home and looking for a little bit of Christian fellowship to give us a new home over Christmas.'

'Say, how about that Scott, can you help these guys please?' said the Officer, who later I found to be the Colonel. Captain Scott, the officer that he had directed us to, heard my story and said that he would be delighted to have a ship on the berth if only to shut the unions up. When I asked when, he said that right now would do just fine.

I called the ship on my mobile and told Jim to warm up his engines; we had a home for Christmas. Two hours later and we were alongside our new berth. There was a very small price to pay, this being that Scott, who was fed up with eating Korean food, would often join us for lunch. We could hear his approach as, always in uniform, his heavy hobnailed boots could be heard stomping along the deck.

By the time Jane arrived we were comfortably tucked up on our new berth and we had an open invitation to visit the Army base and enjoy their facilities. There were three wives aboard for Christmas and New Year and Tito excelled himself in laying on magnificent banquets. Whenever Scott dined with us he would ask to say grace and on the Sunday invited us to attend service at the Army Church. It was a little strange standing up in front of the whole congregation to explain who we were and where we came from.

Now that we were alongside we received many more visits from our Charterers who were most hospitable to the wives and gave us some splendid tours and entertained us regally.

The weather was great when Jane arrived and we were experiencing an unusually sunny spell. One evening around the New Year a crowd of us decided to have a slap up meal ashore in a very smart restaurant that I had been taken to earlier by the British Consul. The interior of the restaurant had glass floor with fish and running water underneath. There was lots of traditional timber decorating the entire place, making it look very old and attractive. I ordered our meal by asking for a traditional Korean banquet. The food was magnificent and plates of food would keep arriving until we were all well satisfied, but only to discover that we had the main course still to come. We had no idea what most of the food was, but treated it as an adventure. The only thing I disliked was raw jellyfish which once in my mouth I could not chew through and had no option but to swallow whole. As it slid down my throat I had a strange drowning sensation. Nobody else was brave enough to try it and I must say I have never had it since.

As we came out of the restaurant we discovered that about six inches of snow had fallen. Everywhere looked very pretty but it became almost impossible to find a taxi to get us back to the ship. As the ladies were hardly dressed for walking we made a dash for the nearest underground entrance. Pusan has a vast network of underground passageways much like Washington DC. Built as an anti-war device they feature shops and other services apart from transport links. We were able to get halfway to our destination where, away from the city centre, the crowds were far fewer in number, and we eventually found ourselves cabs to cover the last few miles home.

When our friends from South Korean Telecom entertained us, it was interesting to notice the different cultural attitude between men and women. Our host on one occasion when approaching his car very reluctantly held the door open for Jane. Drawing in his breath through closed teeth in the oriental fashion, he explained that in Korea the woman usual holds the door open for her husband, and when meeting his wife would she please not mention that he had done this. In fact we were very honoured to be taken back to his house and introduced to his family. Whilst families play a very important role in employer and employee relationships in Korea (houses and schooling are often paid for by the employer), wives and children are not usually introduced into the working environment. His wife was charming and despite being given no notice of our pending arrival produced some delicious fruits and drinks to tempt our taste buds. To our surprise she spoke excellent English when encouraged to talk and we learned that she held a university degree. I think that they were a very unusual couple for Koreans. I wondered if she ever found out about her husband's gallantry towards the English lady!

Later that year we were directed back to Hong Kong for a long overdue refit. Whilst in the dry dock I went to inspect the hull and in the bottom of the dock I met a puzzled Engineering Superintendent and Lloyds Surveyor. They were examining numerous scratches stretching the length of the ship in the antifouling paintwork. The Lloyds Surveyor asked me if we had been aground at all. To their relief I explained the story of our recovering the heavily damaged cable off of Bombay. The scratches would have been caused by the distorted, spiralling cable being dragged along the bottom of the hull. It was however rather unnerving to realise just how shallow the water had been and indeed how close we had been to grounding.

Old ships are usually happy ships. They usually have a character of their very own. Messing around on Christchurch harbour in my old punt I was intrigued with some of the lovely old yachts that visited the harbour. Many of them were echoes from the past. One of my favourite yachts was *Ianthe.* She was only 24 foot long plus bowsprit but she was beautiful. Built at Inman's boatyard in Lymington (now Berthons) during Victorian times for a local landowner she was gaff rigged with a jack-yard topsail. She drew less than a metre with a heavy iron centreplate to compensate for the lack of keel. I would watch her racing up and down the harbour, tacking backwards and forwards across the channel with great precision.

When later I joined the Christchurch Sailing Club I was lucky to be invited to crew aboard *Ianthe.* She was scratch boat in the club handicap system and was always sailed to the limit. When in the spring of 1984 I was standing in the bar at the club quaffing a pint of bitter I overheard the boatman saying that this would be the last year that he launched *Ianthe* I was devastated. His family had looked after the boat ever since she was built in the 1890s. She had been sold to a purchaser from Hamble and would be leaving Christchurch for good.

Determined that this should not happen I apparently put down my full glass of beer and walked out of the club. I drove around to the owner's house and hammered on the door. I knew he was at home by the smoke coming from the boiler in his workshop and just kept banging on the door until he finally appeared. He was not happy as he had been working in the loft and didn't welcome my intrusion, but when I said that I had come to discuss *Ianthe* his mood changed. Owned by the whole family they had tried hard to find a local purchaser for her but to no avail, and they were all very sad at having to see her go. I offered to buy her myself, and after a quick phone call to his daughter, an old crew of mine, we sealed the deal.

Returning to the Sailing Club I picked up my glass and continued the conversation, saying to the other people in the bar 'By the way I have just bought *Ianthe* and she will be staying at Christchurch.'

It took a while for the reality of my new purchase to sink in and with it came the grave concern of whether I could handle this magnificent yacht as previous owners had done without making a pig's ear out of it. She was a wonderful teacher though and I soon got to know her little foibles and peculiarities. I set up a syndicate to ensure that she would remain at Christchurch and today she can still be seen tacking up and down the harbour. Someone once said to me 'One doesn't own *Ianthe.* You are just looking after her for posterity.'

By modern day shipping standards *Iris* was an old lady at the age of twenty, but cable ships seem to go on forever. She had certainly sailed some incredible distances from UK to the Falklands, UK to America and round as far as Bombay, to say nothing of her trip to Bahrain to lay cables in the Persian Gulf.

Whilst in refit at Hong Kong the *Iris* had a change of colour. From the high visibility orange that had given her better recognition in the fog of the North Sea she was transformed into a white lady more suitable to the heat of the tropics. She was quite a sight as I stood on the dockside admiring her.

I was to leave her in Hong Kong and take command of one of the UK based vessels. We had done a lot together and had covered many thousands of miles of ocean. It was with emotions running high that I prepared to leave this funny little ship. Taking one last look around the cabin I picked up my briefcase and headed for the gangway. To my utter surprise and embarrassment I found the entire crew standing at the head of the gangway. Shaking hands with them all brought a big lump to my throat. I wished them all good luck and hoped that they *'may encounter favourable winds and following seas'* as that lovely old man had wished me back in Mumbai.

I returned to the UK for leave and shortly afterwards whilst in command of *Iris*'s sister ship CS *Monarch* I was diagnosed as having Parkinson's disease. This of course came as a terrible blow, but given the wonderful support I had around me and support of the senior management in our company I was able to continue working until I reached retirement age. The Shipping Federation doctor in Southampton (so different from that RN doctor forty years previously), who was also a keen yachtsman, gave me tremendous support and with the help of medication I was able to retain command.

Six months after leaving *Iris* in Hong Kong she completed her Korean charter and was recalled to the UK. I was so proud of that little ship as she sailed into Portland Harbour. In her white paintwork she looked like a swan as she came through the breakwater and berthed next to *Monarch*.

I was invited aboard for drinks and dinner and as I walked up the gangway there was a welcoming committee waiting for me. Having spoken to most of my old crew there was still one person I really needed to see. As I entered the galley my old friend Tito rushed at me and threw his arms around me. The rest of the galley staff were amazed at his demonstrative behaviour. It was truly wonderful to know that I was so welcome on my old ship.

During the evening Ian, the current captain of *Iris*, told me that he felt that he was always walking in my footsteps and that everyone still considered *Iris* as my ship.

He announced that the Company had just secured a contract to put *Iris* on station in the Indian port of Cochin. It was good to know that my efforts in Mumbai had been of benefit and that *Iris* was to have a new lease of life.

Enterprise

Jane and Aaron, aged 4

[illegible]

Crew of *Enterprise*

Enterprise at sea

Ianthe

Ianthe

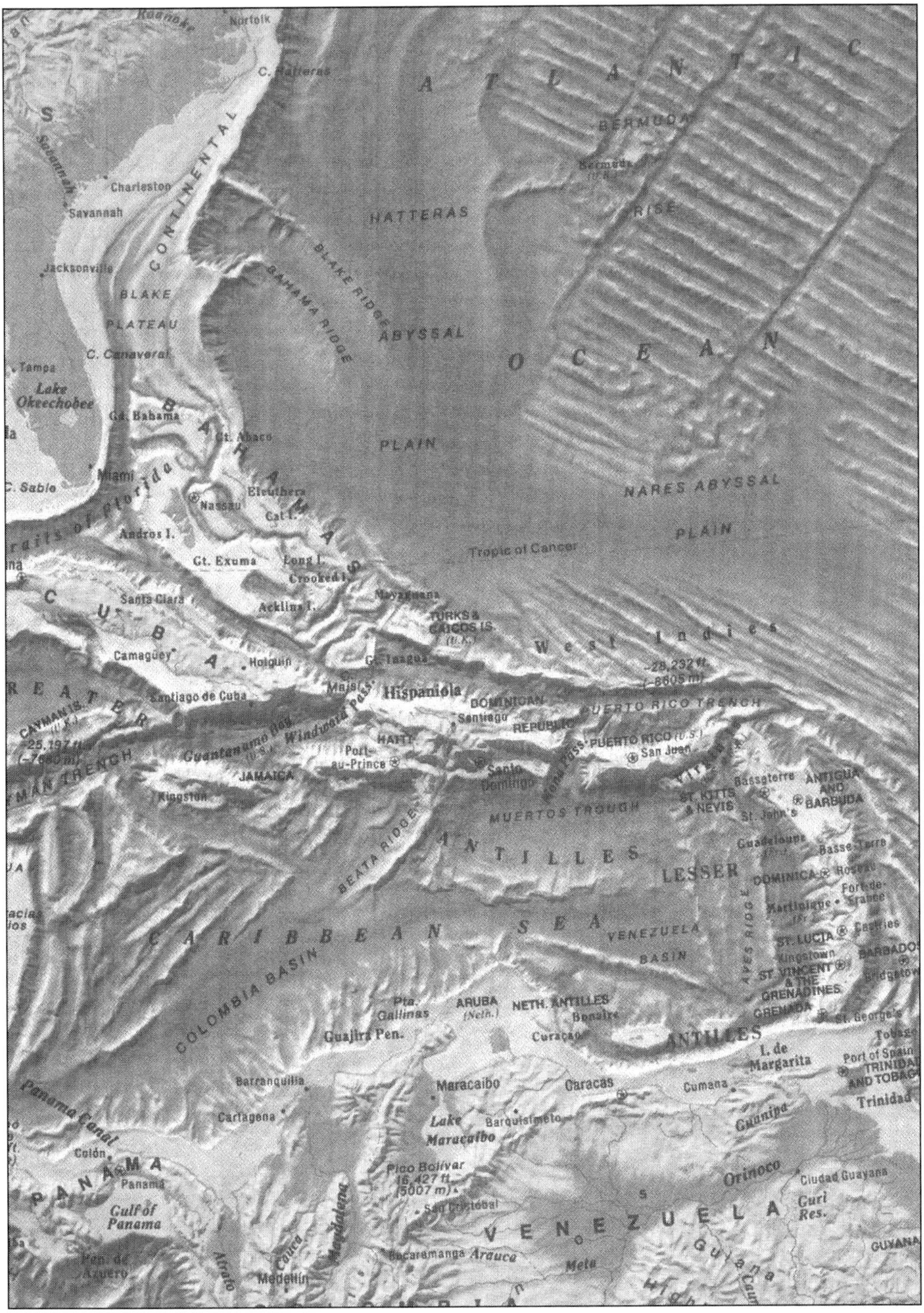

Bermuda to Antigua

Cook Strait

Messing about on the river, Cairo 2007

10

BERMUDA

We were reducing altitude and banking slightly to starboard as I got my first view of the Islands, glistening like a jewel in the deep green waters of the Atlantic. The white lime-washed roofs of the houses dotted amongst the green of the island, fringed with white coral sand and set in the turquoise water is a sight I shall never forget.

We were approaching from the East and I could see my ship lying at her berth in the Old Dockyard.

Bermuda, lat 32°20/N long 64°45/W consists of more than 150 small islands forming a sickle shape, encircling lagoons sounds and shallow reefs, forming about 200 square miles of idyllic sailing waters. Positioned some 560 miles east of Cape Hatteras in North Carolina and on a similar latitude to Madeira they are warmed by the effect of the Gulf Stream, making them the world's most northerly coral islands.

Because of their strategic location, the Bermuda Islands formerly served as the winter naval station for both the British North Atlantic and West Indian squadrons.

The archipelago is littered with wrecks, possibly the most famous of which was Admiral Sir George Somers flagship HMS *Sea Venture* wrecked there in 1609. All the crew survived and when word of the shipwreck and Bermuda's attractions reached England, William Shakespeare used the account of Somers' voyage as the background for his play *The Tempest*.

I was delighted to be returning to Bermuda to take up my command of the Cable Ship *Sir Eric Sharp*. This had been her station since she was commissioned in 1988 and had to be one of the best postings in the fleet. At 6,141 tonnes and 115 metres length she was ideally suited to the North Atlantic. Her compliment of around 70 Officers and crew was made up of some 25 British officers and technicians and around 45 Filipino ratings.

By the time I was through customs and immigration and had collected my bags it was already dark as I climbed aboard a taxi to drive to the other end of the Island to the ship.

The following morning after the formalities of taking over command I walked around the ship taking stock of the situation. We were loading cable from the depot for an installation project in the West Indies.

The Caribbean Islands are knitted together with an array of submarine telecom cables, but one of the links in this chain had been broken when the terminal station on Montserrat had been destroyed by a volcanic eruption. The *Sir Eric Sharp* had earlier in the year recovered most of the cable, creeping close inshore with the air heavy with the smell of sulphur and volcanic ash falling on the decks. Rather a scary and unpleasant business.

Cable and Wireless Marine operated a fleet of over 20 cable-laying and repair ships until the parent company sold CWM to the American company Global Crossings in 1998. As well as a number of dedicated installation vessels we had ships stationed around the world on maintenance agreements. Rather like a fire fighting service these strategically placed vessels were ready on immediate notice to undertake any repairs or modifications needed to the hundreds of thousands of miles of telecommunications cables festooned around the ocean floor.

We were now building a new system aboard the ship to reconnect Antigua and St Kitts and restore the network. The cable had to be neatly coiled by hand into the ship's cavernous cable tanks. Any damaged sections of the recovered cable would need to be cut out and the cable rejointed, a very time-consuming business.

The cable consisted of four pairs of optical fibres surrounded by layers of polyethylene, jute and wire armouring. Each joint of the cable takes a minimum of twelve hours to do and is subjected to rigorous checks and x-rays to ensure its sustainability in the ocean depths.

It would take us another week at least to load the system before we set sail for the Caribbean.

Looking over the side of the ship I could see a bustle of activity around the offshore gangway. Crew were checking and preparing boats for a training excursion. The *Sharp* carried a small flotilla of boats for both recreational and operational use, this of course in addition to the lifeboats. There was a Wayfarer sailing dinghy for the more energetic, an RIB popular with the water skiers, and two cable barges built like mini landing craft and each powered by two large outboards, good for picnics and beach parties plus a 28 foot personnel launch.

The weather was superb and ideal for boating. The whole crew would be working long hours with some heavy work and it was important to give them some fun and relaxation when possible, besides which I would be needing good boat handling skills for the beach landings of the cable in both Antigua and St Kitts.

That day I had received an email from the UK offering me the services of one of our British Boatswains who was waiting for a posting to another vessel. Knowing Steve well I jumped at the opportunity of having him in my team. Hailing from the Falkland Islands he was an expert boat handler with good teaching ability. I knew that his services would be very useful to me in brushing up everyone's boat handling skills, and besides I had another very special task for him!

By the middle of the week we were entertained by the sight of numerous tall ships passing close by before berthing at Hamilton. Bermuda was a stop for them on their race across the Atlantic. Unfortunately there was very little wind and most of them motored in, but even so they made a wonderful sight and gave us a glimpse of how this island must have looked one hundred years ago.

I was expecting a visit from the chairman of our company who was attending a board meeting of our parent company who's registered offices were in Bermuda, and I was expected to host a reception lunch and tour of the Tall Ships. Not wanting anything to go wrong with such illustrious passengers I wanted Steve to prepare the ship's launch and ensure that everything was shipshape and Bristol fashion.

By the time we had nearly completed our load Steve, with a small contingent of ABs, had overhauled all the workboats and their equipment. When launching or recovering boats at sea, even in the calmest conditions, there is always an element of swell which puts terrific stresses on the lifting equipment, and I could guarantee swell in the Outer Windward Islands.

It appeared that the launch, with a top speed of only six knots, was not as popular as the other boats and had not been used much of late. Under the direction of Graham our Chief Engineer she was given a good clean and an engine overhaul, together with a new coat of paint ready for our distinguished visitors.

The reception went exceedingly well with the catering staff excelling themselves and receiving much worthy acclaim. The launch rocked gently at her painter, awaiting her passengers.

The *Eric Sharp*, unlike most modern ships, was fitted with boat booms, wooden spars about 25 feet long and 6 inches diameter attached by goosenecks to the ship's side to hang boats off by. Above the boom the accommodation ladder was secured from a small platform outside the gun port door. Today this is considered rather quaint and old fashioned, but in my opinion very practical and ideally suited to our situation.

With the party safely aboard we set off for Hamilton Harbour. There was a cloudless azure sky and the shallow waters of the Great Sound a magnificent turquoise colour as Steve steered us through the coral reefs.

As we entered Hamilton Harbour the sight before us was truly magnificent.

The Tall Ships, their spars braced round, were berthed three deep along the Waterfront giving a forest of masts and rigging. The ships were a hive of activity with their young crews overhauling the gear after a hard race across the Atlantic from Western Europe and preparing them for their next leg of the race.

Ensigns from all around the world stood out proudly in the light breeze, showing the truly international nature of the gathering. I hope that funding will continue to enable these mighty ships to continue giving such wonderful opportunities to the youth of the world.

After inspecting the fleet we dropped our visitors off in Hamilton and ourselves returned to the ship to prepare for our departure the next morning. We were all rather sad that we would not be there to witness the spectacular departure of the Tall Ships, but our work had to take priority and we had another job to do.

We departed from our berth at 0900 hours the following morning and set on for Antigua, a distance of about 920 miles to the south.

As I read through the voyage plan prepared by the Third Mate I was amused to read that we were heading into – The Bermuda Triangle!

Our plan of operation for the cable lay was, with the ship holding station about three cables off the beach, the cable end would be towed ashore, with floats attached to keep it on the surface. Once sufficient cable was ashore the end would be anchored and jointed to the land cable. Once the joint was completed and the cable tested through satisfactorily the ship would move off, paying out cable along the chosen previously surveyed route. Once halfway across to St Kitts the cable end would be sealed and lowered to the seabed and buoyed off. The cable had been prepared in two sections to accommodate this.

The ship would then proceed to St Kitts and repeat the operation back out to the cable buoy which would be recovered and the two ends of the cable jointed together and lowered to the seabed and released.

Two days previously we had received bad news that the jointing team expected to fly out to the West Indies were no longer available. Their work and expertise were crucial to the success of our operation as they were to have jointed the sea cable to the land cable once we had floated the cable ends ashore.

Our senior onboard jointer Dave was expecting to retire and was already nearly one month overdue his release. His relief was due to arrive before our departure from Bermuda. With a new plan in my mind I summoned Dave to my cabin. I could tell that he was suspicious and his opening words were, 'If you are going to tell me that I have to stay on, forget it Skipper. My wife would kill me.' Sitting him down I unfolded my plan. I wanted Dave to fly down to Antigua to supervise the landing, but suggested that his wife would join him there and continue on to St Kitts where, once our work was completed, they would be free to have a holiday to celebrate his retirement. This of course would be at the expense of the Company. With this news, Dave left me to telephone home and seek his wife's agreement. I don't think she took much persuading!

The ship carried a submersible known by her build number as Sub128, together with a full operating team, as part of our standard equipment. As we were not expecting to use the sub the team asked to be involved in the cable landing operation. Always pleased to have willing volunteers they would form part of the boat team during both beach landings.

Three days after leaving Bermuda and without serious incident we arrived off St John's the capital of Antigua and picked up the local pilot before going alongside. As we arrived the Miami Weather Bureau announced that a TRS (tropical revolving storm) was forming to the east of the Islands. I was anxious to get started and be away before the hurricane arrived.

We had equipment to land, meetings to be held with the local Cable & Wireless representative, and I wanted to see the landing site for myself.

We left the berth at first light and moved around to the cable landing. I backed the ship into position and set the DP (dynamic positioning) system to hold the ship on station whilst the cable was floated ashore. This was where the boat skills came into the fore. Once the cable end had been towed ashore and secured, the floatation bags secured to the cable at 4–5 metre intervals had to be cut free and the cable allowed to drop gently to the seabed. Even with the ship only three cables off the beach there would be at least 150 floats to recover. Fortunately this was the leeward side of the island with little swell. St Kitts would be very different though.

By midnight things were progressing well and in the early hours of the morning with the cable testing through to satisfactory limits we moved off, paying out cable over the stern. With the ship moving comfortably we made about six knots and reached the mid point between the islands by the afternoon. After sealing the end of the cable, ground tackle was connected and then moorings equivalent to the depth of water to ensure that the buoy didn't move. We slipped the buoy before dusk and set on for Basseterre on the West coast of St Kitts, where we anchored off the town shortly after sunrise.

The port had sustained serious damage from a hurricane the year before and most of the quays were still out of action. Going ashore by launch with the ship's purser we completed all the official paperwork with customs and immigration. I met up with the local C&W guys and we went off to inspect the landing site.

The beach landing was giving me concerns. Being on the eastern side of the island it faced out into the Atlantic and there was always surf running onto the beach. A lot of time and effort is spent on surveying cable routes to ensure that the cable is well positioned and free from danger. The route had been surveyed right into the shore but the corridor was very narrow. I had suspicions that there were reefs extending offshore but not shown on the charts. I had arranged to hire a local fishing vessel and sent two of my Navigating Officers off to conduct our own survey. Using the boats GPS and echo sounders backed up by horizontal sextant angles and a hand lead they soon reported back that a four metre patch did extend up to nearly eight cables offshore and very close to the cable route. This meant that I would have to position the ship at least one mile off the beach, which with the additional problems of the surf and currents would make the landing of the cable even more difficult. As there was little information available on tides and currents the survey team had positioned several poly buoys with a string of small pellets attached offshore. With a man positioned on some nearby high ground armed with a pair of binoculars we were able to record the tidal movement and times of slack water.

Returning to the ship we departed the anchorage that evening and arrived off the beach at first light. All of our planning paid off and we had the cable end ashore by breakfast with only a few wet shirts from the 128 team. The cable pulled by the tide had taken on a strong bow to the south and several of the boats were needed to hold the floating cable back. As our recorded time of slack water approached we prepared to cut the floats and let the cable rest on the seabed. I was very relieved to see right on cue the bow slowly come out of the cable and I gave the order to start cutting floats away. I know that I had given my crew a hard time over the additional survey work but the end result was well worth all the effort. It is thorough planning and attention to detail that makes this work a success. The sea is a tough mistress and after more than 40 years at sea I am always prepared to learn from her ways.

Once again Dave showed his worth and completed the beach joint in good time and in the early hours of the morning with all the boats and crew safely back onboard we commenced laying cable.

With the seabed seldom flat it is necessary to pay out the exact amount of cable to fill in the contours of the bottom. Insufficient slack in the cable would result in suspensions whilst too much would allow the cable to throw loops. These loops if tightened would result in kinks in the cable and the cable being inoperable. As we left the shore the seabed dropped to several hundred metres. To achieve the necessary control we had some very sophisticated computer programmes linked into the navigation suite and fed data from the cable engines. On this occasion we were trialing a new system in parallel to our standard kit. This kit was operated by a team of boffins who had flown out from the UK to assist us.

With about ten miles of cable paid out, the whole navigation system collapsed, resulting in excess cable being paid out. I stopped the ship and waited for test result from the Cable Engineers. Sure enough the test result reflected my fears and two of the fibres had gone down. We had no choice but to recover cable. After one mile had been picked up we found two tight kinks in the cable. Cutting out the damaged section the cable was jointed and proved once again intact. This time much to the chagrin of the boffins I insisted that the new equipment was disconnected before we continued. There is a time and a place for development of these highly sophisticated systems and this was not the one.

After a delay of nearly 24 hours we eventually arrived at the buoyed cable end. Overlaying the buoy by the required distance we cut the onboard cable and transferred the end to the bows. Recovering the overlay we then recovered the buoyed end and commenced our final joint.

Another twenty-four hours saw us slipping the cable bight over the bows. With all systems testing perfectly we were free to leave the cable ground and return to Bermuda.

We called briefly at Basseterre to recover some equipment, to clear out from Customs and to pick up some fresh provisions that the Purser had ordered. I was eager to get clear of the islands and away from the threat of hurricanes.

During the morning watch the next day the Chief Engineer became concerned with the high sea temperatures. We relied on seawater to provide cooling for not only the main engines but also for the air-conditioning and power generating plants. When the sea temperature reached above 30 Celsius the situation became quite serious. Reducing speed and shutting down as much equipment like radars, laundry and computers as possible, we altered course to the East in search of cooler water. We were clearly in the Gulf Stream a strong current, which empties tropically heated water out of the Gulf of Mexico through a relatively narrow channel between Florida and Cuba. Its speed and breadth vary considerably, with currents of up to five knots at times as it makes its way up the eastern seaboard of the United States.

Fortunately we soon reached the eastern edge of the current and the sea temperature dropped over 5 degrees in less than one hour. This phenomenon can be quite alarming to unsuspecting newcomers to these waters, and I was reminded of the Third Mate's caution in his voyage plan about the Bermuda Triangle.

Once more we were making good speed towards the ship's home port. When the Purser arrived at my cabin with some coconuts still wrapped in their outer husks and some sugar cane that he had acquired for my son I was reminded that my wife and six year old son would be joining me in Bermuda.

I had arranged for them to be collected from the airport and taken to an hotel on the southern side of the Island. On the morning of our return to base I was up early and pacing the deck, imagining my family having breakfast and looking out to sea to watch Daddy's ship come over the horizon. We were reunited later in the day and both my wife and son had a truly magical holiday. The time difference between Bermuda and London gave me the opportunity to get up early and do most of my work before lunch, freeing me up to enjoy the afternoon boating and swimming with them.

Towards the end of their stay, I had arranged a trip in the launch across the sound to the old capital of St George's. Graham the Chief Engineer and Steve the Boatswain had prepared the launch with provisions, including a good supply of cold beers. Checking communications with the duty officer on the bridge we set off on our exploration. It was a beautifully clear day with radiant sunshine and smooth sea and we were about half way across the Sound when to my alarm the engine made strange noises and with steam emitting from the engine box it came to a full stop. Having great faith in Graham I was not unduly perturbed, until he announced that the lube oil pump had collapsed and there was no spare aboard. I just counted my lucky stars that this hadn't happened when all the VIPs were onboard. We could do nothing but anchor and call the ship for a tow. I had always made it a standard rule that whenever any of the boats were away from the ship a rescue crew must be on standby. Unfortunately our hand-held VHF radio was out of range and the launch's larger set was powered from the main engine. Feeling very sheepish I resigned myself to having to wait for a passing boat to give us assistance.

Graham in his very laidback fashion announced that he was going to teach my son to fish. Producing some frozen squid out of the icebox he was casually washing it over the side when my wife said he should be careful that he wasn't attracting sharks. Stating that there were no sharks in these waters, Graham was mortified when the bait was taken out of his fingers by a baby reef shark, much to my son's amusement.

Suddenly the radio burst into life with 'Launch, launch this is rescue 128. Do you require assistance?' You can imagine my relief to hear those welcome words. At least it showed that my standing orders were being followed and that the duty officer had proved his training. He had kept a weather eye on our passage and seen our dilemma. As the rescue boat, manned by our indomitable submersible team, rounded up and stood a boat's length away we were held to ransom. They were all dressed up like pirates brandishing makeshift cutlasses. 'If you want a tow back, Skipper, it will cost you all the beer in your icebox . . .' was their demand. My son thought this was great fun and truly in the spirit of 'Pirates of the Caribbean'. Willingly I paid up and accepted the ignominy of a tow. This was the climax of a wonderful holiday for a six-year-old boy.

11

NEW ZEALAND

It was with a little sadness that I waved good-bye to Jane and Aaron at the airport in Bermuda. It had been a wonderful holiday for them both and my son didn't want to go home but wanted instead to stay with his Daddy. Who could blame him for wanting to stay there in Bermuda with its warm turquoise blue waters to play in. However I was leaving the *Sir Eric Sharp* to fly to New Zealand to join her sister ship the *Pacific Guardian.*

That morning I had received news that an important cable crossing the Cook Strait had gone faulty and that we were tasked to repair it. This cable operation was one that I did not relish. Some six months earlier I had been in Command of the *Guardian* and hosted a meeting with the cable owners and other interested parties to formulate a plan for repairing this cable should the scenario occur. There had been a repair made to the same cable some two years before, when things had gone horribly wrong and the repair had taken nearly two weeks to complete.

The Cook Strait is one of the most notorious stretches of water in the world. The Strait separates North and South Islands of New Zealand and besides having extremely strong tides the weather can change very quickly and dramatically. The mountain ranges of New Zealand separate two different and diverse weather complexes. Dave, my Purser on the *Eric Sharp,* only the previous day as we sat around the dinner table enjoying a glass of port, had been recounting his experiences when, as a young purser, he had been aboard the ill fated ferry *Wahini* that had been overcome by a sudden storm and was wrecked at the entrance to Wellington harbour with considerable loss of life. The following account is gleaned from 'New Zealand Disasters' in Christchurch City Libraries.

- On the morning of 10 April, 1968, Cyclone Giselle hit Wellington at the same time as another storm which had driven up the West Coast of the South Island from Antarctica. The two storms met over the capital city, creating a single storm just as the inter-island ferry *Wahine* was crossing Cook Strait.

- The *Wahine* had left Lyttelton at 8:40 pm the night before, carrying 610 passengers and 123 crew. There had been storm warnings, but nothing to say that this storm would be any worse than other winds in the strait well known for its rough seas.
- The ferry travelled up the east coast of the South Island and headed for Wellington Harbour. By now the winds were gusting at between 130 and 150 kilometres per hour.
- At 5:50 am on the morning of 10 April the captain of the *Wahine*, Captain Hector Robertson, decided to enter the harbour.
- Twenty minutes later the ferry was alongside Pencarrow Head. The winds had increased to 160 kilometres per hour, and those on board could only see for a distance of 800 metres. On board the *Wahine* the radar system was no longer working.
- A huge wave pushed the *Wahine* off course and in line with Barrett Reef, and the captain was unable to turn back on course. The force of another massive wave threw him across the bridge of the ship.
- He decided to keep turning the ferry and try to bring the *Wahine* around and back out to sea again. For 30 minutes the *Wahine* fought the waves, but by 6:40 am had been driven back onto the rocks of Barrett Reef.
- Most of the passengers did not realise that the ferry had struck rocks because they could tell little difference between that impact and the battering the ship was receiving.
- Captain Robertson ordered the closing of all watertight doors and dropped both anchors when he learnt that none of the engines was working.
- Passengers were told that the ferry was aground on the reef, and to put on their lifejackets and report to their assembly points around the ship.
- The accident was reported to the signal station at Beacon Hill, just above Point Dorset, and the crew prepared the life-saving equipment. Flooding was reported in four compartments and the vehicle deck, which could affect the stability of the ship.
- As the intensity and power of the storm grew, the winds increased, and the *Wahine* dragged its anchors. At this stage the weather was so bad that no help could be given from the harbour or the shore.
- Gradually the *Wahine* drifted further down the harbour, until she was just by Steeple Rock, off Point Dorset. By now a tug had set off from Queens Wharf to try and reach the *Wahine*.
- At about 11:00 am a line from the tug was used to try and tow the ferry, but the line gave way. Other attempts failed, but the deputy

harbourmaster managed to climb aboard the *Wahine* from the pilot launch which had also reached the scene.

- At about 1:15 pm the combined effect of the tide and the storm swung the *Wahine* round so that there was a patch of clear water sheltered from the wind and the sea on the starboard side. This was on the side towards which the ferry was leaning more and more.
- Captain Robertson had not considered abandoning the ship earlier because he felt it was safer for the passengers to remain on board, given the storm conditions. But now the order was given to abandon ship.
- Passengers, not told before how serious the situation was, were now confused and frightened. People slid across the sloping deck, trying to make their way to the lifeboats.
- Only the four starboard lifeboats could be launched, and crewmen tried to get as many people as possible onto them. One lifeboat was swamped when it hit the water and people were lost into the sea. Some managed to hold onto the boat as it drifted across the harbour to the eastern shore.
- Some people tried to make their own way ashore, jumping from the *Wahine*'s decks. Others reached the inflatable life rafts which had been thrown overboard, but several of these were punctured in the wreckage.
- The waves of the sea were still battering the ferry, and people in the water struggled to keep hold of wreckage or the sides of the lifeboats.
- The captain and deputy harbour master were the last to leave after checking that no one remained on the ferry. They were in the water just by the wreck for an hour before being rescued.
- At about 2:30 pm the *Wahine* rolled completely onto her side. By then the first of the survivors were reaching the shore at Seatoun.
- Rescuers there helped the passengers ashore, not realising the extent of the disaster. Other survivors drifted across the harbour to Eastbourne, where over 200 survivors eventually landed.
- The road to Eastbourne had been blocked by a slip, and rescue teams were delayed in reaching the coast, but were there in time for the flood of people who struggled through the surf to safety.
- 51 people died in the disaster, most of them middle-aged or elderly.

Knowing the unpredictability of the weather, especially as we were in the middle of their southern winter, I could expect only a very short weather window for conducting the repair. Planning to make provision for all eventualities was essential. That meeting six months before had given me an excellent feel for the problems we were likely to encounter.

I had flown out from the UK to Auckland in January 2001 and it had been my first visit to New Zealand since those troubled days on the *Chupra* some thirty-five years before. I had been somewhat reluctant to travel to literally the other side of the world at that moment, as my wife and I were about to complete the legalities of adopting our son Aaron. Personnel however had promised to bring me home for the all important court hearing. There was a certain degree of déjà vu about returning to New Zealand and I hoped that my trust in Personnel and their promises was not misplaced.

I was absolutely elated to discover, on my arrival in Auckland, that they were in the midst of the America's Cup yachting races. The elimination races had finished and they were winding up to the final races to select the challenger from competitors from around the world. The New Zealanders were of course the holders at that time and I was amazed at the public support given to the local team. It was as if the entire country had America's Cup fever. The Local Television coverage was superb with magnificent graphics that could show to within a metre which yacht was in the lead, even when they were hundreds of metres apart on different tacks.

The *Pacific Guardian* was the maintenance ship for cables in the South Pacific an area ranging from Australia to Hawaii. She normally shared her time between Australia, New Zealand and Fiji but on this occasion was having a prolonged stay in Auckland. The America's Cup races covered an area through which several highly strategic cables lay, and the fact that these cables carried the media reports of the races to avid followers around the world meant the Cable Owners had asked that the ship remain in Auckland throughout the race period. This of course suited me very well and I was feasted to a surfeit of top yachting activity. I even got to sail aboard and even helm one of the yachts. This was an incredible experience for me. The yacht was so responsive and because of her deep winged keel could turn on a sixpence. When tacking as she came through the wind and bore away one could feel the acceleration as the sails filled. We were berthed only a couple of hundred yards from the newly built marina which housed not only the competing yachts but a wonderful collection of super yachts from around the world. I was in my element.

I had hoped to meet up with my friends from my BI days who had been so hospitable to me all those years before. Unfortunately I had lost all contact with them and had even forgotten their names. When I was visited by the chairman of the local Master Mariners Club, seeking a ship visit for his members, I told him of my dilemma. Surprisingly he was an ex-BI man himself and only a couple of days later I was amazed to get a telephone call from him giving me the names and telephone number of my friends. When I called, Anne's reply was 'How on earth am I expected to remember a visitor from thirty-five years ago? Just a moment whilst I look in our Guest Book.' There sure enough was my entry for December 1967. She was so excited and later that day I met up with Anne and Tony. They were very interested in my ship and I was so pleased to be able to entertain them aboard.

The crew of the *Guardian* were Fijian and astounded me in their size, strength and dexterity. They looked as if they would be more at home on a rugby field, and in fact many of them had played Rugby for their country. In Fiji young boys begin playing rugby using a coconut as a ball. No wonder they have such good hands at catching the ball. One slip with a coconut could result in broken fingers. They were very much into their sport and in fact one of our cooks had been caddy to a famous international Fijian golfer. They made up an excellent crew and were always singing. They were colourful gentle giants.

I was very pleased on my arrival to find my old friend Jim there as Chief Engineer. We had been through all manner of difficult times together and it was good to be reunited. It was thanks to Jim that I had my sail on the yacht. This had been a very special birthday present from him.

The day that the local yacht beat the American Challenger the whole country seemed to go wild. There were parties everywhere and downtown Auckland was just one massive fiesta. It's great to see a country that supports its sportsmen and women to such an extent.

That same day my relief arrived to enable me to fly home to attend the court hearing. My trust had not been misplaced and three days later I was on my way back to Auckland with the wonderful knowledge that Aaron was now really our son.

When the yachting came to its conclusion we moved across to Devonport (on the other side of Auckland Harbour) for our annual dry-docking and refit that included the fitting of a Dynamic Positioning System. As my cabin positioned as it was under the bridge was in shambles because of all the new cable runs etc., I was living ashore during the early part of the refit.

One morning as I came up the gangway I could tell that all was not right. As I reached my cabin I was met by the Third Mate who informed me that the police had been aboard. There had been an incident ashore the previous evening when a woman had been attacked by a Fijian seaman with a broken bottle. They suspected that the seaman was one of my crew. We had always had excellent relations with the authorities and this type of behaviour was the last thing I wanted.

I summoned the Bosun to my office and said that I wanted the culprit to identify himself, and in the mean time all shore leave was cancelled. I was amazed when half an hour later a young seaman of about twenty, who I shall call Robert, came to my office and admitted that he was the person responsible. I was bitterly disappointed as I had high expectations of Robert and had considered sponsoring him for an Officer Cadetship. He said that he could remember very little of the incident but said that he was just defending himself and had picked up the bottle which was already broken and had done no more than threaten the woman with it. I told him that he would need to go to the police station, and as he turned to leave the office I noticed him wince.

Asking him what was wrong he told me that he had been cut on his side. There was blood seeping from an open wound. Instructing the Third Mate to take him ashore to the hospital, I then contacted the police. The police were treating the matter very seriously as I expected. The courts in New Zealand are very tough on the Islanders, that is people from the South Pacific, and I suspected that Robert would get a prison sentence and later be banned from entering New Zealand subsequently. Within the hour the Third Mate returned saying that the police had arrested Robert and taken him into custody. The report from the hospital was that that the wound had been made by a knife and had penetrated several inches into his buttock.

The ship's carpenter came to see me and said that he had been a witness to the incident and that they had been sat outside a pub having a quiet beer when the woman had approached Robert and provoked an argument. He had seen her lunge at Robert who had tried to defend himself. I had strong belief in my crew and was certain that Robert would not have initiated a fight. Although I could never condone a man attacking a woman I could understand that given such provocation it would be very difficult not to react. I called our agents and asked for a lawyer to meet me at the police station. One hour later we were talking to the Chief Inspector. The sergeant who had made the arrest had not been aware of the knife wound but admitted that the woman had a record of attacks of this nature especially against Fijians.

Robert's case was due to be heard that afternoon. The police sergeant was happy to drop the charge but because of its severity it still had to go before the Magistrate. Sitting in the court I felt very conspicuous in my white tropical uniform and reflected on the other court that I had attended in England only one week before.

The solicitor did a sterling job and I was asked to give a character reference and be responsible for Robert's behaviour, to which I willingly agreed.

The Magistrate acquitted Robert and he was asked to make a donation to a charity. We waited outside in the lobby of the court for him to be put through the procedures. When he appeared with a police officer he looked very worried, frightened and bemused. It took Chippy several minutes to explain to him that he was not going to jail and was free to return to the ship. When he finally got the message he threw his arms around me.

I subsequently heard that the woman was arrested and charged with assault. Robert had been a lucky young man and I don't think he will ever forget that experience.

My flight from Bermuda to Auckland was not the most pleasant experience. The first two legs from Bermuda to Miami and then LA were with American Airlines. Even though my ticket was business class the flights were uncomfortable and the service poor. Although I was only in transit I was put through the full immigration and customs checks. Believing that I had completed the correct forms I waited patiently in the queue, only to be told when I reached the head of the queue that I had the wrong form. Taking the proffered new form I went to a desk and did my best to fill it in. Once completed I was told to rejoin the queue at the back. When once again I reached the front of the queue I said to the stroppy immigration Officer 'Before you send me back for another form, perhaps you can advise me if there are any more of your precious forms I will require.' 'No sir,' she said in a very tight voice, 'that will be all thank you.' I don't know where they recruit the US immigration staff from but they certainly can be most unpleasant. I was just very relieved that from LA I was flying Quantas.

Since my earlier sojourn aboard the *Pacific Guardian* she had undergone some fairly extensive trials for her new DP system. Never in favour of retrofit systems on ships I was rather sceptical as to the DPS ability to hold station in the Cook Straits if things turned nasty. We sailed from Auckland the day after my arrival and I was glad to take the opportunity whilst on passage of putting the new equipment through its paces. Arriving in Wellington we were given the best passenger berth in the centre of town. We had a couple of days to check and prepare our selves before loading the repair cable which involved shifting to another berth.

The cable owners who also had two very high voltage power cables running across the Straits had a team of patrol boats and divers on full time patrol. The manager of the team, whom I had met six months earlier, met us on arrival in Wellington. We had an instant mutual respect and understanding that made working together easy. He had his helicopter on stand-by to take me on a tour of the Straits that was extremely useful. From the chopper I had an impressive view of the turbulent waters of the Straits with huge tidal swirls and vicious over-falls in places.

We landed in a small bay where we were met by an outboard dinghy that ferried us out to the dive boat. They had located one end of the broken cable but the divers were limited to only twenty minutes on every change of tide. We don't usually use divers on a cable repair but with this one I was grateful for all the assistance I could get.

Normally we would grapple for the cable ends and once hooked bring the end to the surface where we would remove any damage and having sealed the end slip the cable on a buoy. My problems here, apart from weather constraints, were that the broken cable ends were lying very close to the High Voltage Power Cables and we knew from previous experience that our normal rigid cable buoys would be towed under by the strong tides and implode in the water pressure. My plan was for the divers to locate the two ends then weight the ends and attach a thin line with a poly buoy, which would be towed under by the tide but would break surface during slack water at the change of tide. The problem with this idea was finding a rope thin enough (less than one inch diameter) yet strong enough to lift the cable. We were lucky to find some one-inch Kevlar rope in a local yacht chandlers.

My plan was that once both cable ends had been located and buoyed the *Guardian* would pick up one end and secure a heavy composite line to it then, paying out on that line, move across to pick up the second end. I knew that we would only have about twenty minutes of slack water whilst the buoys were on the surface. Once both ends were secured we could make our first splice between the seaward end and the stock cable. On completion of this first joint we would pay out on the stock cable, recovering the heavy compound rope until sufficient of the second end was onboard. The stock could then be cut and the two ends joined together.

In anticipation of a fault on this cable I had arranged for a section of cable to be shipped to Auckland to give our jointers opportunity to practise jointing this cable. The cable was quite different from our normal optical fibre cable and required different procedures and techniques. Planning was crucial if this repair was to be done without the problems encountered previously.

As the time for neap tides approached we moved across to the storage depot to load the stock cable. The loading completed we waited for the tide, weather and the divers to complete their work. Studying the weather forecasts it looked as if we might get our break right on the neap tides, and as soon as I received word from the divers that they had successfully buoyed both ends we sailed. As we backed out from the berth into Wellington harbour, the pilot drew my attention to a large house on the hillside with panoramic views of the whole harbour. He informed me that this was the home of Jonah Lomu the famous Kiwi rugby player. New Zealand certainly looked after their sporting heroes.

Once out in the Straits we just had to wait for the slack water. All manner of thoughts ran through my mind. We had onboard a number of people representing the Cable owners and their insurers. They all wanted a piece of the action and congregated on the bridge. All manner of misgivings crossed my mind as the tension built up. Had my planning been right? Were we going to get the weather? Had the divers attached the thin Kevlar rope correctly? With my nerves jumping I was so relieved to see the first buoy break surface. The divers boat raced in and lifted the buoy as I manoeuvred the ship in to put the dive boat under our bows. With ten minutes gone we had the end of the Kevlar on board and every pair of eyes on the bridge was searching for the second buoy. Just as I was beginning to doubt my plan the buoy popped up. And the dive boat moved in. Cautiously I moved the ship across and the end was passed up to the foredeck. With both ends now captured we were ready to commence the repair.

Now we just had to wait for the Cable Engineers to make all their tests and for the jointers to join up the cable ends. The first trial joint had taken several days but with practice they had considerably reduced this. Every six hours the tide would turn and I couldn't trust the new DP system to hold station with the tide coming from astern and the cable at the bow. I was planning to turn the ship on each change of tide but we had to swing back through the same quadrant each time or we would put a twist in the cable that would cause a fault in the fibres. This was why the weather was so crucial. If the wind shifted the wrong way I would have difficulty in pushing the stern through the wind.

Trying to keep all of my misgivings and forebodings from showing, I handed the control of the ship over to the duty watch and retired to my cabin.

The weather was good to me and the jointers did a fantastic job. Twenty-seven hours after we had sighted that first buoy the second joint was completed and the Chief Officer payed out the cable bight as I cautiously backed the ship away. It had been a tremendous success of planning and teamwork. Returning to Wellington there was jubilation aboard, especially from the Cable owners who asked for a celebratory party. Once the ship was secured at the berth I took myself away to my cabin and release my emotions. Sitting in my chair I felt utterly drained. I had expended so much nervous energy and been living on adrenalin such that my body just needed to recover. The troubles associated with stress I find are not encountered at the time of the pressure but afterwards when the body needs to recharge its batteries. I remember sitting there in my chair with tears running down my face. It had taken a lot out of me but I had proved to myself that I could still do it.

After half an hour's rest I showered and donning clean uniform went out to join in the partying. My team had given me so much that they all needed and deserved to celebrate. That night as I lay in my bunk I could hear the wind howling in the rigging outside. We had been very lucky as once again Wellington lived up to its reputation of being 'The Windy City.'

Three months later I left the *Guardian* in Newcastle NSW and on my last night the crew gave me a farewell party the memory of which I shall always treasure. The Fijian's were in fine voice and sang me their farewell song *Isa lai* (see p 131). I was presented with a Tapa cloak made from the bark of the mulberry tree and worn by Chiefs. It was a very touching gesture and epitomised these lovely generous people.

12

THE AUTUMN YEARS

With retirement in the offing my last ship was to be the *Cable Enterprise*. Built in 1964 she was a very elegant ship and looked rather like a yacht with raking masts wooden decks and gleaming white paintwork. It was rather fitting that the oldest captain had the oldest ship, as we were both looking to retire at the same time and I am only sorry that I didn't get to bring the old lady home to the UK before we parted company, she to the breaker's yard and me to the lovely rural countryside of Dorset.

I joined her in Victoria, British Columbia, a place that was another favourite of mine. I had spent some happy times there whilst in command of the *Seaspread*, the vessel that we had met up with in the South Atlantic several years before. *Seaspread* had been bought by Cable and Wireless and converted into a cable layer. Having originally been built as a dive support vessel she had lots of reserve power and thrusters, which would keep her on station in the roughest conditions.

Victoria being both the capital of Vancouver Island and British Columbia was a great place to be stationed. Jane and Aaron had visited me there and we have good memories of driving around the beautiful island and staying overnight at the ski lodge where we all three had our first taste of skiing. Just before our visit to the ski slopes there had been heavy snow falls giving the area forty feet of snow, which is hard to imagine and was quite awe inspiring as we drove up the approach road to the resort with the snow banked up on either side of the road. Aaron, who was only four at the time, can remember having dinner with some friends of mine and having to slide down a slope of ice to reach their front door, normally approached by a set of steps going upwards.

I had only been on the *Enterprise* for a few weeks when I slipped in the shower and ended up in hospital with a severely sprained back. After a week in hospital I was flown home first class British Airways. That was an experience in itself.

After a couple of month's recuperation I rejoined *Enterprise* in the Caribbean where she had taken up station in Panama. Having flown out to Curacao in the Dutch Antilles where we had loaded cable we returned to Panama that was to become our base. I remember that journey as we sailed through the blue waters of the Caribbean along the Venezuelan coast. My mind was taken back to all the boyhood books of piracy that I had been so fond of. This was the Spanish Main and I thought of Captain Hornblower fighting pirates in these same waters. It was a splendid feeling pacing the deck, feeling the ship rise to the light swell and looking at the blue waters speckled with white horses. This was the life that I had dreamed of. To be Captain of my own ship sailing through waters steeped in so much romantic history was heaven.

Enterprise being an old ship was very heavy on man-power, especially in the catering department. Fortunately as the galley and dining saloon were on different decks it was not convenient to introduce self-service catering and I was pleased to retain the silver service that was such a feature of this lovely old lady.

In line with the catering, I insisted on retaining the dress code for Officers in the evening. Between the hours of six and nine, Officers would dress in Red Sea Rig when attending either the mess or dining saloon. This may seem a trifle draconian and a few of them showed surprise on first joining the ship, but very soon agreed that it was a nice rather quaint tradition and well worth retaining.

During that last year at sea, I was lucky to be able to give Jane and Aaron a holiday in Panama. They travelled out via Miami and had a few days on the ship before I took local leave and we went off to our holiday destination that I had discovered on the Caribbean coast of Panama.

We were picked up in Panama City by a mini-bus that took us across the isthmus to the North coast and then to the East. The road became more and more rutted until we finally left the tarmac behind and continued on a gravel road. The land is very fertile there and their fence building methods intrigued me. The farmers would cut a branch from a tree and just stick it in the ground as a post where it would grow and soon become a tree. This gave excellent shade to the animals in the fierce tropical sun.

The mini-bus finally pulled off the road at a tiny village where two small wooden finger jetties protruded out into the sea. As the driver unloaded our bags and placed them aboard a boat that was little more than a canoe powered by an outboard engine, Jane started to have reservations. Assuring her that all was well we climbed aboard our new transport. A young lad not much more than a teenager steered us seaward towards the off-lying island of Isla Grande. Steering round the western end of the Island we started to encounter some swell and with the tiny boat rising and falling on the swell, Jane became seriously alarmed.

Suddenly the coast opened up to reveal a deliriously pretty bay with a collection of little yellow painted chalets surrounding a swimming pool and open-air bar and restaurant. It was absolutely delightful with a backdrop of rainforest and banana trees.

Not surprisingly the complex was called the Bananas Hotel.

We had a truly magical relaxing holiday there and after she had overcome her initial misgivings Jane agreed to us going on a boat excursion with a young American couple to the old port of Portobello. Aaron loved clambering over the ruins of what at one time had been the most heavily fortified city on the Spanish Main. That is until it had been ransacked by Captain Henry Morgan, who was clearly Aaron's hero until replaced by Jack Sparrow!

That was a wonderful holiday. After leaving Isla Grande we returned to Panama City and enjoyed many wonderful and unusual tourist sights such as the Ship Canal and tree-top walks through the rainforest canopy. We visited native villages in the jungle where the people seemed totally unspoiled by the attention of tourists. Through our guide and interpreter Aaron was able to ask all manner of questions about their habitat and lifestyle, which I think will live with him for many years.

The Tourist Board in Panama City had built three villages on high ground behind the old city. They depicted life in the three communities.

(a) The Spanish Conquistadors with their tiled roofs.
(b) The Negroid Caribbean with corrugated iron houses, and
(c) The Native Panamanian Indians with houses made from rushes and straw.

Aaron was fascinated by the different ways of life but especially I shall remember him looking across at the modern-day city and all its slums and saying. 'We are so lucky aren't we Daddy, to live in a nice house with its garden when these poor people have nothing.' For a child of seven these were prophetic words indeed.

I was ever mindful of our ambassadorial status whilst stationed in a foreign port and when the lads arranged a football match against the local Expats I was eager to encourage them. This became a regular weekly feature and when I was approached to host a charity evening I joyfully gave my support. The evening was attended by the British Consul, European Expats and members of the local Filipino Community. With a splendid barbecue followed by shipboard horse racing and frog racing we raised over two thousand dollars that, with advice from the Consul and with Aaron's words ringing in my ears, we gladly donated to a local school for street children.

The response from the school was amazing and we were all so touched by their work that it was decided to hold a Children's Christmas Party. Everybody on board became involved and when the coach arrived carrying some twenty children it was wonderful to see their faces. These children, picked up daily from the streets of Panama City and many of whom were homeless, had never before seen such bounty. I was particularly amazed when as they were each given a little goody bag to take home they quickly emptied the bags of toys and party poppers and replaced them with fruit to take home to their families. An apple and an orange meant little to us but to those kids it was the world. Every member of the ship's company had been involved and all had a huge lump in their throats as the children left the ship. As I walked with them to the bus, the driver came up to me and with tears running down his face threw his arms around me and thanked me for what we had done. To us it was a small thing but to those children it was huge.

It was a few months after our holiday that I retired and was given a marvellous send off by my crew, with a sumptuous farewell dinner that I shall always treasure the memory of.

People ask if I miss the life. Yes of course I do. I miss the support and company of my crew, especially those long dinners where we would sit and chat over the Stilton whilst passing the port around the table.

Yes I have thoroughly enjoyed my career at sea, from being a brass bound apprentice on little ships carrying fruit home from the Mediterranean to the climax of being in command of a highly complex and sophisticated cable ship with a crew numbering in the sixties.

Having carried cargoes as diverse as waste paper to Corfu and potatoes from Ibiza; I have seen the challenge of having to stow a thousand tons of oranges on top of a few army trucks and taken home the Captain's special oranges.

I have sailed with passengers ranging from the very affluent, travelling first class from Cape Town to Southampton, to the poor Hindu families travelling the Gulf in search of work with their total possessions wrapped up in a few bundles.

I joined the might of the British Navy mobilised to defend far-off parts of what was once the British Empire. I can honestly say that I have travelled the world.

I have always tried to support my staff and not take anyone for granted. People's thirst for knowledge should be encouraged and I have always endeavoured to avoid the idiom of 'the need to know basis'. The more one's staff know, the better they are equipped to support you, and the easier is the task in hand.

I owe so much to my parents and my family for supporting me throughout my career. It has been a great life and most rewarding. I hope that when Aaron reads these memoirs he will gather something from them. The sea and people who sail on it have many unique qualities. Neither should be taken for granted. I have tried to learn from my experiences and have never stopped learning. I remember an old Captain once saying to me 'keep your vents well trimmed and a weather eye open at all times, my lad.'

EPILOGUE

As I walk around my garden I reflect back on the fullness of my life and recognise how lucky I have been. I had the most wonderful parents and a loving family who have supported me throughout my life. I have been able to follow the career of my choice and I have met some very interesting people. My two daughters have given me four adorable grandchildren, although I must admit to not being the most attentive of grandfathers.

From my teenage years I have fought to conquer the affliction of speech impediment, only to have it return in later life as a side effect of Parkinson's disease. I was recently shown a cutting from the *New York Times* that has helped me come to terms with my returning speech impediment. Whilst the various Parkinson's Specialists who I have seen have assured me that there is no relationship between stuttering and Parkinson's, Dr Maguire, a psychiatrist at the University of California, has suggested that people who stutter produce an excess of dopamine. As it is a lack of dopamine that is responsible for the effects of Parkinson's it may well follow that the drugs given to sufferers to increase their dopamine levels could cause stuttering in some patients. Whilst this revelation has not cured my affliction, understanding the reasons for it is of tremendous benefit.

I started to write these memoirs to keep my mind from growing stagnant in retirement. It all stated one morning whilst driving Aaron to school. A chance remark of 'Daddy, you have so many stories that you should write a book,' was the catalyst that I needed. They started off as just a few scribbles and jottings and have grown somewhat in both content and volume. I have found it most rewarding to look back on all those events that have filled my horizons.

Jane and Aaron have given me their absolute support and the energy to continue to live a full and purposeful life despite adversity. I am resigned to the fact that I am no longer able to participate in sailing and boating and I regret that I am unable to pass on to Aaron the pleasures of just messing about in boats. He is a tremendous character and fills our lives with his laughter and joy.

A couple of years ago we acquired our golden retriever who we called Bosun, that I thought had suitable nautical connections, and he keeps us all agile. To watch Aaron and Bosun playing together is a delight. The dog follows him everywhere and they are clearly the best of friends.

Living deep in the English countryside as we do, Bosun ensures that we get out to enjoy walking through the fields and woods, through all the seasons come rain or shine. He is great at springing deer and pheasants although I am sure he would never harm anything should he catch it. He is just a big white fluffy ball of fun who keeps us all amused even when he comes home after rolling in something unmentionable.

There have been certain pillars in my life; people who through their tacit support have given me courage and conviction. My sister Anne was always there for me during my childhood. My old friend Jim has not only been a good chief engineer but has always been a great listener. When I first introduced Jane to my mother she told me that she had been determined not to like the girl but she did. They became very close friends right up to the day that Mum passed away and I know how lucky I have been to have her support and love, even if at times I don't show it.

ISA LAI
FIJIAN FAREWELL SONG

Isa isa valagi lasa dina
Nomu lako au na rarawa kina
Cava beka ko a mai cakava
Nomu lako au na sega ni lasa.

CHORUS

Isa lai, na noqu rarawa
Ni ko sa na vodo e na mataka
Bau nanama, na nadatou lasa
Sonaisali nanuma tiko ga.
Vanua rogo na nomuni vanua
Kena ca ni levu tu na ua
Lomacqu voli me'u bau butuka
Tovolea ke balavu na bula
Domoni dina na nomu yanuyanu
Kena kay wale na salsalu
Mocelolo, Bua, na Kukuwatu
Lagakali, Maba na rosi damu.

* * *

Isa, Isa, you are my only treasure
Must you leave me, so lonely and forsaken?

As the roses will miss the sun at dawning,
Every moment my heart for you is yearning.

CHORUS

Isa Lei, the purple shadow falling,
Sad the morrow will dawn upon my sorrow;
O forget not, when you're far away,
Precious moments at Sonaisali

Isa, Isa my heart was filled with pleasure,
From the moment I heard your tender greeting;
Mid the sunshine, we spent the hours together,
Now so swiftly those happy hours are fleeting

O'er the ocean your island home is calling,
Happy country where roses bloom and splendour;
O if I could but journey there beside you
Then forever my heart would sing in rapture.